Christian Baptism

By

Adoniram Judson

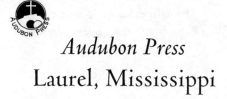

Audubon Press
Laurel, Mississippi

AUDUBON PRESS
2601 Audubon Drive ❖ P.O. Box 8055
Laurel, MS 39441-8000

Orders/Inquiries: 800/405-3788
Voice: 601/649-8570 ❖ Fax: 601/649-8571
E-mail: *audubon@c-gate.net*
Web Page: *http://www.c-gate.net/~audubon*

All Scripture quotations are from the *King James Version*.

Contents

Foreword

Adoniram Judson (1788-1850), a virtual legend in his own time, has been all but forgotten by a new generation of Christians. We care little for biography today. We care even less for missionary biography. Our less is great. This is especially true in regards to the person and work of Adoniram Judson, America's first Baptist missionary.

Judson, born into the family of a Congregational clergyman in Massachusetts, entered Brown University at the age of sixteen, with sophomore standing. By 1807, at the age of nineteen, he had graduated as valedictorian of his class. He then taught school, wrote two textbooks on grammar and mathematics, and spent a brief time in New York City as a skeptic and aspiring playwright.

By 1808, still unsure of his faith, he entered Andover Theological Seminary. Amazingly, at least when one considers what happens to many who enter seminaries in unbelief in our day, Judson was soon converted. He committed himself, shortly afterwards, to foreign missions service. Joining with the famous Williams College group of alumni (Samuel Mills, James Richards, Luther Rice, and Gordon Hall) who were also students at Andover, he helped to found a missionary agency.

On February 6, 1812, Judson was ordained a Congregationalist minister. He sailed for Calcutta on February 19. While on board ship a very unusual thing happened. Judson, ever an extremely gifted linguist and student of the Greek text of the New Testament, came to view adult baptism by immersion as the clear teaching of the New Covenant. Judson had to carefully and soberly count the cost of what he had discovered and the result was that he embraced decidedly Baptist beliefs. Upon arriving in India, Judson and his wife Ann submitted to believer's baptism at the hands of the famous pioneer Baptist missionary, William Carey. American

Baptists soon adopted the Judsons as their first foreign missionaries, and the rest of the story is a tale of great faith and continued courage.

This present volume, long out of print, is actually a very long sermon (on Matthew 28:19) preached prior to Judson's receiving his own baptism in India in 1812. It includes an interesting letter to Judson's church in Plymouth, Massachusetts, as well as collection of quotations that Judson assembled to show the arguments of those who practiced infant baptism. It also includes a short address on the mode of baptism. I believe that this reprinted edition is valuable for several reasons.

First, this is a careful, wise, and well written work. Judson cuts right to the heart of the issue. He knew the opposing viewpoint well, having ardently held it. He most assuredly does not misrepresent the views of paedobaptists in his disagreement with them. This is an irenic and eminently fair polemical work. It serves, in this sense, as a model for us right down to the present time.

Second, this little volume shows very clearly how Judson came to his beliefs and specifically how the text convinced him to change his mind. Judson knew the importance of words and their meanings. He was a serious student of texts, contexts, and word meanings. In our time few seriously debate the issue in this manner. Judson does and will thus be a help to earnest readers of the Bible.

Third, because we are seeing a wide-scaled recovery of Reformation theology in our time, for which I give great praise to God, many are again considering the place of the sacraments in the life of the church and the Christian. This concern for the sacraments, both their meaning and importance, is healthy. It also leads us back into some issues seriously considered in the past. Our forefathers wrestled with these practices mightily. They often did not agree but they did know how to make a case for their convictions that was well thought out. Judson is a model of such. As one who is convinced that the views Judson held regarding baptism are correct, I believe this little book will prove to be extremely useful to a new generation.

Finally, Judson was a man of great conviction and courage. It was not easy for him to come to the views he adopted. Think of the cost. He had to begin his efforts from the ground up. Yet he was willing to be faithful to what he saw in the New Testament. Regardless of whether or not you agree with Judson, you would be well served to take his manner of approach, both to the issue and to the truth. Whatever you see in the text of Scripture, obey it and stand by your conviction no matter what. You will, thereby, not have regrets. God will honor his truth in your life as He did in Adoniram Judson's.

John H. Armstrong, President
Reformation & Revival Ministries
Carol Stream, Illinois

Preface

When I first became acquainted with the life of Adoniram Judson and especially with his book *Christian Baptism*,[1] it became apparent that the time had come again for the story of his pilgrimage from paedobaptism to professor's baptism to be told. Indeed, no other time since its last American edition was printed over 150 years ago, has needed its republication as much as our own. The reason for this has been due in large part to the amazing recovery of the reformed faith in the past fifty years.[2] Literally, as it were, overnight, many reformed Christian book publishers have arisen (especially, in the last twenty years) and have brought many great books written by many great men of yesteryear back from the dead. In such times, ministers find great spiritual nourishment and at the same time new spiritual heroes. Men that speak their language, men who speak of a deeper experience and communion with the living God that they themselves have yearned for, men who knew the hand of God upon their ministries. For many ministers this is their first

---

[1]It was through my good friend Erroll Hulse that I first learned about the existence of this rare book. For a very brief yet helpful, description of the life of Judson, see Erroll Hulse's paper entitled, *Adoniram Judson — Devoted for Life* (Westminster Conference Papers - 1994: *Building on a Sure Foundation*, pp.123-156), or for an expanded version of this paper, see Erroll Hulse's book entitled, *Adoniram Judson and the Missionary Call* (Pensacola: Chapel Library, 1996).

[2]For a clear description of this wonderful movement of God in our own generation, see both the excellent booklet written by Robert Oliver entitled, *A Glorious Heritage: The Recovery of the Reformed Faith in Twentieth Century England* (London: The Evangelical Library, 1997), and the article by Erroll Hulse entitled, *The Theological Renewal 1950-2000* (Reformation Today #162, pp.17-24).

encounter with vital Christianity, and it has come to them through books written by men from another age very much unlike their own.

As wonderful as this new discovery is and its subsequent effects upon a man of God, it does not relinquish his need to still examine everything carefully (1 Thess 5:21), even from men whose feet you feel unworthy to wash. In other words, we must always be on guard so as to not feel that we have to buy the whole bag of a theological system or of a man's teaching without having first allowed it to simmer for a good while in our thinking.

Sadly, however, this process has not been the practice of many Baptist brethren, both young and old, in their consideration of the reformers' and puritans' theology. Instead, they have been enamored by it and have fallen prey to the type of covenant theology[3] adhered to by our paedobaptist brethren. It is our hope that this reprint will cause our reforming Baptist brethren, as well as cause our former baptist brethren to reconsider their theological shift and hopefully embrace the sound covenant theology so clearly portrayed by Adoniram Judson.

Originally published by William Carey's Serampore press in 1813, it subsequently went through five American editions.[4] This edition

---

[3] Judson's Covenant Theology was one with his congregationalist brethren except on the single point of baptism [See Iain H. Murray's *Revival and Revivalism* (Carlisle, PA: The Banner of Truth Trust, 1994), p. 316 and also David B. Calhoun's *Princeton Seminary* (Carlisle, PA: The Banner of Truth Trust, 1996, 2 vols.), 2:467, endnote 13].

[4] The subsequent American editions were reprinted in the following years: The first and second (both in 1817. Incidentally, Judson's aging Congregationalist father was dismissed from his pastorate on account of his change to believer's baptism after reading one of these editions [William B. Sprague, ed. *Annals of*

is taken from the 5ᵗʰ American edition of 1846. The editing of this edition has been kept to a minimum and consists mainly in some updating to contemporary spelling and punctuation. None of the original text has been omitted.

Of course, bringing this work to print has not been without the assistance of many. Therefore, I wish to give thanks to two of my faithful sisters in Christ, Mrs. Sharon Williams for typing the manuscript and Miss Bethany Morgan for the initial proofreading of the original. In addition, I would like to thank the following individuals: Pastor Jeff Gage for his timely assistance in the final stages of this project, Tom Haverly, Librarian of the Colgate-Rochester Divinity School Library, Mrs. Sharon James, Dr. Richard Belcher, and the Evangelical Library of England for the photographs, Bob Ross of Pilgrim Publications for Spurgeon's appendix on baptism, and my dear brother Erroll Hulse for his patient, persistent encouragement to finish this project. Last, but certainly never least, I wish to thank my wonderful wife Dawn and our seven children, who both sacrificially and consistently encourage their husband and father in the work of the Kingdom!

Jerry Marcellino, Pastor
Audubon Drive Bible Church
Laurel, Mississippi

---

the *American Pulpit* (New York: Robert Carter and Brothers, 1860, 9 vols.) 6:607]), the third (in 1819), the fourth (in 1832), and the fifth (in 1846).

Introduction

Adoniram Judson's life and ministry has had an enormous impact on Burma (now called Myanmar). This nation has a population of about 47 million, 63% percent of which is Burmese, representing the strongest Buddhist body in the world. There are reputed to be over one million pagodas (or Buddhist temples) in the country. About 87 percent of the entire population (Burmese and tribal) is Buddhist in religion.[5] It was to this land, then a one hundred percent monolithic stronghold for Buddhism, that Adoniram and Anne Judson sought to bring the Gospel. To that one single purpose they were dedicated for life, and for that cause they laid down their lives.

As I show in my biography *Adoniram Judson and the Missionary Call*,[6] the obstacles were, humanly speaking, insuperable. Credit must be given to Felix Carey, son of the famous English pioneer missionary William Carey, who worked in Burma before Judson and who established an invaluable base from which Judson was able to operate. The story in the early years was about gaining a foothold. Today there are many Baptist churches in Burma totaling over half a million members. The majority of these are believers from the tribal peoples, Kachin, Chin, Karen, Lisu, Lahu and Mara, who inhabit the outer perimeters of the country while the main central area is occupied by the Burmese. It was the great burden of Adoniram Judson to reach the Burmese people. In the event the Karen people in particular responded more readily to Judson and his fellow

---

[5]Patrick Johnstone, *Operation World* (Lawrenceville, GA: OM Publishing, 1993) 398-400.

[6]Erroll Hulse, *Adoniram Judson and the Missionary Call* (Pensacola: Chapel Library, 1996).

missionaries. Progress among the Burmese was very gradual. It has been so ever since although today, more than ever before, progress is being made. It is noteworthy that the Baptists vastly outnumber other Christian denominations in Burma.[7] It is even more extraordinary that that fact can be traced largely to what went on in Judson's mind during the protracted sea voyage to Burma.

In his diary Judson describes that experience which is recorded in this book. The epic two volume biography by Francis Wayland[8] also contains the chronicle. The challenge that confronted Judson at that time was critical and urgent. In his future mission how should he regard converts? More particularly how should he regard the children of those converted? Should he follow the principle of the Abrahamic covenant? If a tribal chief was converted should he baptise him as well as his wives, children and the tribal members? Judson's narration of how he thought through the principles provides a valuable synopsis of his position on baptism.

The method followed by Judson was to consider first the meaning or mode of baptism, and second the subjects. This logical order was to be followed by another contemporary, Alexander Carson (1776-1844), a well known Irish Presbyterian minister and scholar whose conversion to

---

[7]Ibid, *Operation World*, 398.

[8]Francis Wayland, *Memoir of the Life and Labours of the Rev. Adoniram Judson, D.D.* (London: James Nisbet & Co., 1853, 2 Vols.). These two volumes can be borrowed from *The Evangelical Library*, 78A Chiltern Street, London, W1M 2HB The United Kingdom

the Baptist position created a great stir at the time.[9] Carson first wrote a 168 page exposition on the mode of baptism and followed with 70 pages on the subjects of baptism. Readers will see that Judson's consideration of mode fills 32 pages while 115 are devoted to the subjects of baptism.

Are these arguments relevant today? Indeed they are. With regard to mode, Judson is excellent in his treatment and thorough in his references. He hesitates when it comes to the practical arrangements required to immerse 3,000 converts in Jerusalem on the day of Pentecost. A contemporary Australian Presbyterian minister became convinced of the Baptist position while in Israel doing archaeological research. In 1989 he wrote up his findings on the Miqva'ot, Jewish immersion pools for purification, which would have provided all that was needed for Christian immersions.[10] That is an advance on Judson's knowledge. Regarding the subjects of baptism Judson proceeds to the central issue of the covenant. That today is the principal matter of debate. The difference between the Mosaic Covenant and the New Covenant is that the former embraced a whole nation while the latter includes only those who evidence the writing of the law of the Lord on their minds and hearts. The continuity and discontinuity in the administration of the Covenant of Grace is the hinge on which the matter of subjects for baptism turns. Judson opens up what the administration of the covenant with Abraham meant of him personally, and what it pointed to for the future. More detailed and

---

[9]Alexander Carson, *Baptism: Its Mode and Subjects* (Grand Rapids: Kregel Publications, nd, reprint [1853]).

[10]Murray Adamthwaite, *Baptism is Immersion!* (Reformation Today #109, pp.30-40).

precise expositions of the covenant administration as understood by Baptists are available today[11] but Judson argued the case with lucidity.

A change of position on this foundational subject was enormously costly to Judson. He would lose all his support. His wife (and they were newly married), made it clear that she had no intention of changing her views on the matter. However, when she prayerfully studied his exposition she too became convinced. It did cost the couple dearly. However, at about the same time, their associate Luther Rice came independently to the same conclusions. There was no telephone or e-mail correspondence then. Providentially, ill health compelled Luther Rice to return to America where he became a herald for Judson's cause and raised the support essential for his mission.

On the way to Burma, Judson visited William Carey at his mission station at Serampore, India. There he requested believer's baptism. At that time he preached on the subject. Carey described his exposition as the best he had ever heard. It was Carey who urged the publication of this work. It is well that he did, for by taking up the timely republication of that work we can be better informed on a subject which is always made more relevant when there are converts to Christ. How is the union of believers to be expressed? Judson will tell you.

Erroll Hulse, Associate Pastor
Leeds Reformed Baptist Church
Leeds, England

---

[11]Paul K Jewett, *Infant Baptism and the Covenant of Grace* (Grand Rapids: Eerdmans, 1978) and Erroll Hulse, *The Testimony of Baptism* (Leeds, UK: Carey Publications, 1982).

Christian Baptism

A Sermon
on
Christian Baptism,

with many quotations from paedobaptist authors.
To which are added a letter to the church
in Plymouth, Mass., and an address on
the mode of baptizing.

By
Adoniram Judson, Jun. A.M.

Fifth American Edition.
Revised and Enlarged by the Author

Boston: Gould, Kendall & Lincoln.
59 Washington Street.
1846.

Entered according to Act of Congress, in the year 1846, by
Gould, Kendall & Lincoln,
in the clerk's office of the district of Massachusetts.

Part I
What Is Baptism?

Matthew 28:19 — *"Go ye therefore, and teach all nations, baptizing them in the name of the Father, and of the Son, and of the Holy Ghost."*

When our Lord commissioned his disciples to proselyte all nations, he instituted the sacred ordinance of baptism. The words of the institution suggest two inquiries: *What is baptism?* and, *To whom is baptism to be administered?*

Had the Greek word, which denotes the act of baptizing, been translated in the English version of the New Testament, there would probably have been among English readers no dispute concerning its import. Had either of the English words, wash or sprinkle, or immerse, been substituted for the Greek word, an English reader would instantly conceive an appropriate meaning. But, unhappily, our translators have retained the original word, and contented themselves with merely changing its termination. Thus, an English reader is deprived of his usual guide. There are no other applications of the word, in his own language, from which he can learn its import. The only expedient, therefore, of which he can avail himself, is to ascertain the import of the original word: and to this end, the following considerations may conduce.

1. The primitive word bapto *from which the word denoting baptism is derived signifies immersion.*

This, with the general consent of the Paedobaptists themselves, is as much the appropriate meaning of the Greek word, as of the English word, *dip* or *immerse*.[12] This is the word used in the New Testament, when the rich man entreats that Lazarus may be sent to *dip* the tip of his finger in water:[13] when Christ says, "He it is, to whom I shall give a sop, when I have *dipped* it;"[14] and when, in the Revelation, Christ is represented, as clothed with a vesture *dipped* in blood.[15] The inspired penmen have used no other word, beside this and its derivatives, to convey the idea of immersion; nor have they ever used this word in any other sense.

The word denoting baptism, *baptizo*, is derived from the verbal of this primitive word *baptos* by a change in the termination, which, according to an established principle in the Greek language, never affects the primary idea; but when made on words, expressing a quality or attribute, merely conveys the additional idea of *causing* or *making*.

Thus the Greek word, which signifies *pure*, with this change of termination, signifies *to make pure*. The Greek word, which signifies

---

[12]Dr. Worcester said, "Had it been the intention of the Savior, to confine his followers to dipping or immersion, the proper word to express this ordinance, would have been, not *baptizo*, but *bapto*." *Letters to Dr. Baldwin, Let. xxii. p. 125.*

Mr. Buck said, "They (the Paedobaptists), believe, that the word *bapto*, signifies to dip or to plunge; but that the term *baptizo*, which is only a derivative of *bapto*,..." &c. *Theol. Dict. Art. Bapt.*

[13]Luke 16:24

[14]John 13:26

[15]Rev. 19:13

sprinkled, with this change of termination, signifies *to make sprinkled,* or *to sprinkle.* And the Greek word, which signifies *immersed,* with this change of termination, signifies *to make immersed,* or *to immerse.*[16]

Accordingly, that eminent Greek critic, Dr. Campbell, expressly pronounces the primitive and the derivative to be synonymous.[17]

---

[16]There is no position more frequently maintained by modern Paedobaptist writers, than that *baptizo* is a diminutive of *bapto.* But there is certainly no position more untenable, and more perfectly destitute of all support from standard philologists and Greek classics. The termination *-izo* in Greek derivatives, is of the same import, as the termination *-fy,* in English derivatives, from the Latin *-fio,* to make; as, *sanctify,* to make holy, from *sanctus,* holy; *mollify,* to soften, from *mollis,* soft, etc. And derivatives are thus formed, not only from adjectives and neuter verbs, but also from the verbals of transitive verbs; as *aireo* - to choose; *airetos* - chosen; *airetizo* - to make chosen, to choose; *emphaino* - to show; *emphaines* - shown; *emphanizo* - to make shown, to show; *kathairo* - to cleanse; *katharos* - clean; *katharizo* - to make clean, to cleanse; *raino* - to sprinkle; *rantos* - sprinkled; *rantizo* - to make sprinkled, to sprinkle. And according to the same analogy; *bapto* - to immerse; *baptos* - immersed; *baptizo* - to make immersed, to immerse. It follows, therefore, that verbs in *-izo* derived from the verbals of transitive verbs, are, with scarcely any exceptions, of the same import as their roots.

[17]*Four Gospels,* Note on Matt 10:22. See also, to the same purpose BECKMANNUS, *Exercit. Theolog. Ex. xvii* p. 257; BURMANNUS, *Synops. Theolog.* Loc. xliii. c. vi. & 2; SUICERUS, *Thesaur. Eccles.* Sub voce *baptisma;*

2. The word which denotes the act of baptizing, according to the usage of Greek writers, uniformly signifies or implies immersion.

It is the word used in the Septuagint translation of the Old Testament to express the action of Naaman when he *dipped* himself seven times in Jordan.[18] It is the word used by Josephus to convey the idea of immersion; in describing the death of one who was drowned in a pool by order of Herod;[19] and by the same author, in instances too numerous to be detailed.[20]

It is the word used by Porphyry, in mentioning a river, in which an offender on entering, is immediately immersed up to the head.[21]

TURRETTINUS, Institut. Loc. xix. Quaest. xi. & 4; HEIDEGGERUS. *Corpus. Theolog. Christ.* Loc. xxv. & 21.

[18]2 Kings 5:14

[19]*Antiq. Jud.* L.xv.C.iii. & 3

[20]*Antiq. Jud.* L.iv.C.iv. & 6; *De Bell. Jud.* L.iv.C.iii. & 3; *Vita,* & 3; and as quoted by Dr.D. Scott, L.i.C.xxii. & 2; L.i.C.xxvii. & i; L. ii.C.xviii. & 4; L. ii.C.xx. & 1; L.iii.C.ix. & 3; L. iii.C. x. & 9.

[21]*De Styge,* p. 282. In regard to this and similar instances, which are sometimes adduced, by Paedobaptist writers, it is to be observed that the word *baptizo* conveys the simple idea of immersion, whether partial or total. Restricting clauses may teach us that it is partial; the absence of such clauses, and perhaps collateral circumstances, may teach us that it is total. If Christ had commanded his disciples to be

Numerous instances may be produced from other Greek authors to confirm this signification.[22]

Nor has any instance been produced in which the word, literally applied, does not denote *immersion*, or *washing* by *immersion*. In figurative applications, this word, like the English words *dip* and *immerse*, and like all other words, is probably used with some freedom. But should a few instances of this kind be found, would they be sufficient to invalidate the force of evidence resulting from the proper and general use of the word? What law will bind a subject, if he is at liberty to depart from the proper and general interpretation of the principal term, and affix to it a signification, which is drawn from some rare figurative application? Had the rite of baptism been prescribed in the English language, and the word *dip* been used to express the act, could we have entertained a doubt concerning the meaning? And in what light should we regard an attempt to prove that it has no definite import, but signifies sprinkling, or any kind of wetting, because Dr. Johnson defines the word, 1. *To immerse*; 2.

---

immersed up to the head, he would have commanded a partial immersion; but since he has commanded them to be immersed, without adding any restricting clause, we infer the necessity of total immersion. The same can be inferred from other circumstances. See the first quotation from Dr. Wall, under the eighth particular of the 1st part.

[22]STRABO, L.vi p. 84; L.xii. p. 391; L.xiv. p. 458; Dro, xxxvii. p. 64; xxxviii. p. 84; I. p. 492; POLYB. L. iii. C. lxxii; L.v.C. xlvii; PLUTARCH, DE *Superstit.* Tom. ii. Op. f. 166; DIODORUS SICULUS, L. i. C. xxxvi. L. i. C. lxxiii; L. xvi. C. lxxx; HELIODORUS, L. v. 197; AESCHYLUS, *Prometh. Vinct.* p. 53; ARIST. *de Mirab. Auscult.* p. 87.

To moisten, to wet; and in proof of the latter meaning cites these lines of Milton:

> "And tho' not mortal, yet a cold shuddering dew *Dips* me all over?"[23]

If this principle of interpretation be allowed, it will destroy the force of every command. That immersion is the *native* and *proper* signification of the word *baptizo,* is so universally asserted by all lexicographers and critics, that no one scarcely presumes to deny it; and to attempt to prove this point, by citing authorities, would be quite preposterous.[24]

That immersion is the *exclusive* signification of the word appears from the following testimonies of eminent Paedobaptist authors, whose concessions on this subject could not have been affected by Baptist partialities, but must have resulted from a conviction of truth alone.[25]

---

[23]This figurative application of the word *dip*, finely illustrates the application of the word *bapto* in the Septuagint translation of the prophecy of Daniel, where it is said that the body of Nebuchadnezzar was dipt in the dew of heaven.

[24]But as a specimen, SEE VALESIUS, *Annot.* in Euseb. *Hist. Excles.* L. vi. C. xliii. p. 120; LEIGH, *Critica Sacra,* sub voce; CALVIN, *Instit.* L. iv. C. xv. & 19; WITSIUS, *(Econ. Faed.* L. iv. C. xvi. & 13.

[25]If it be asked why these learned men still practiced pouring or sprinkling, one of their number shall inform us: CALVIN. "It is certain, that we want nothing which maketh to the substance of baptism. Wherefore, the church did

8

BUDDAEUS. "The words *baptizein* and *baptismos* are not to be interpreted of aspersion, but *always* of immersion."[26]

ALSTEDIUS. "*Baptizein, to baptize,* signifies *only* to immerse, not wash, except by consequence."[27]

J.J. WETSTENIUS. "To baptize is to plunge, to dip. The body, or part of the body, *being under water,* is said to be baptized."[28]

J. ALTINGIUS. "For baptism is immersion, when the whole body is immersed; but the term baptism is *never* used concerning aspersion."[29]

BEZA. "Christ commanded us to be baptized, by which word, it is certain, immersion is signified. Nor does *baptizein* signify to wash, except by consequence; for it properly signifies to immerse for the sake of dyeing. To be baptized in water signifies *no other* than to be immersed in water, which is the external ceremony of baptism."[30]

LUTHER. "The term *baptism* is a Greek word. It may be rendered immersion, as when we plunge something in water, that it may be entirely

---

grant herself liberty, since the beginning, to change the rites somewhat, except the substance." Comment. in Acts 8:38, in Baldwin's *Series of Letters,* p. 201.

[26]*Theolog. Dogmat.* L. v. C. i. & 5.

[27]*Lexicon Thelolg.* C. xii. p. 221.

[28]*Comment.* ad Matt. 3:6.

[29]*Comment.* ad Heb. 9:10.

[30]*Epist. ii. ad. Thom. Tilium. Annot.* in Mark 7:4, and Acts 19:3.

covered with water. And though that custom is now abolished among the generality (for even children are not entirely immersed, but only have a little water poured on them;), nevertheless, they ought to be completely immersed, and immediately drawn out. *For the etymology of the word evidently requires it.*"[31]

CASAUBON. "This was the rite of baptizing, that persons were plunged into the water; which the very word *baptizein, to baptize,* sufficiently declares."[32]

CATTENBURGH. "In baptism the whole body is ordered to be immersed."[33]

KECKERMANNUS. "We cannot deny that the first institution of baptism consisted in immersion, and not sprinkling."[34]

SALMASIUS. [35]"Thus Novatian, when sick, received baptism, being *perichutheis, sprinkled,* not *baptistheis, baptized.* Euseb. vi. Hist. C. xliii."[36]

---

[31]*Opera,* Tom. i. p. 72. Wit. 1582.

[32]*Annot. in Matt.* 3:6.

[33]*Spicileg. Theolog.* L. iv. C. lxiv. Sect. ii. & 22.

[34]*System. Theolog.* L. iii. C. viii. p. 369.

[35]Dr. Johnson. "Salmasius was a man of skill in languages, knowledge of antiquity, and sagacity of emendatory criticism, almost exceeding all hope of human attainment." *Life of Milton,* p. 75.

[36]Apud Witsii *AEcon. Faed.* L. iv. C. xvi. & 13.

DR. CAMPBELL. "The word *baptizein*, both in sacred authors, and in classical, signifies *to dip, to plunge, to immerse;* and was rendered by Tertullian, the oldest of the Latin fathers, *tingere,* the term used for dyeing cloth, which was by immersion. *It is always construed suitably to this meaning.* Thus, it is *en udati, en to jordane.* But I should not lay much stress on the preposition *en,* which, answering to the Hebrew *b,* may denote *with,* as well as *in,* did not the whole phraseology, in regard to this ceremony, concur in evincing the same thing. Had *baptizo* been here employed in the sense of *raino, I sprinkle* (which, as far as I know, it never is, in any use, sacred or classical), the expression would doubtless have been,"etc.[37]

"When, therefore, the Greek word *baptizo* is adopted, I may say, rather than translated into modern languages, the mode of construction ought to be preserved, so far as may conduce to suggest its original import. It is to be regretted that we have so much evidence, that even good and learned men allow their judgments to be warped by the sentiments and customs of the sect which they prefer. The true partisan of whatever denomination, always inclines to correct the diction of the Spirit by that of the party."[38]

---

[37]The two verbs, rendered *wash,* in the English translation, are different in the original. The first is *nipsontai,* properly translated *wash;* the second is *baptisontai,* which limits us to a particular mode of washing; for *baptizo* denotes *to plunge, to dip.* "Baptizesthai," says that excellent critic (Wetstein) "est manus aquae immergere, *niptesthai,* manibus affundere" (*Note* on Mark 7:3-4).

[38]*Four Gospels,* Note on Matt. 3:11.

3. There are no instances in the New Testament which require us to depart from the etymological and established interpretation of the word.

We must believe that the writers of the New Testament used words according to their usual acceptation in the Greek language, unless the connection requires some other interpretation. If we suppose that they used words in a manner different from common, established use, without giving sufficient intimation, either expressly or by the obvious scope of the passage, we must give up our only guide to the meaning of any word, or charge them with a design of misleading. They certainly knew that their readers would naturally and necessarily interpret every word in the usual way, unless taught differently by the connection.

Let us examine those instances in which it has been supposed that the connection renders the idea of immersion inadmissible.

It is said that we cannot suppose that the washings (according to the Greek, *baptisms*) of cups, and pots, and brazen vessels, and tables, or those ablutions which the Jews practiced before eating, were all done by immersion.[39]

With regard to the former, it must be remembered, that the Jews were commanded, in their law, to cleanse unclean vessels by immersing them; "whether it be any vessel of wood, or raiment, or skin, or sack, whatsoever vessel it be, wherein any work is done, *it must be put into water.*"[40]What is more probable, than that they abused the first institution of this ceremony, by superstitiously immersing a variety of articles not included in the divine command?

---

[39]Mark 7:3-4.

[40]Lev. 11:32.

That the Jews, on returning from market, immersed themselves before eating, may appear improbable to an inhabitant of the north of Europe or America; but not to you, my brethren, who are acquainted with the customs of these eastern countries, and witness the frequent ceremonial immersion of the natives.

But that these baptisms were really immersions, and, therefore, that the use of the word, in these instances, instead of weakening, must confirm the belief that it always means immersion, appears from the following testimonies.

GROTIUS. "They cleansed themselves from defilement contracted in the market, not by washing the hands merely, but by immersing the body."[41]

SCALIGER. "The more superstitious part of them (the Jews), every day, before they sat down to meat, dipped the whole body. Hence the Pharisee's admiration at Christ, Luke 11:38."[42]

RABBI MAIMONIDES. "Wherever in the law, washing of the flesh or of the clothes is mentioned, it means nothing else than the dipping of the whole body in a laver; for if any man dips himself all over, except the tip of his little finger, he is still in his uncleanness."[43]

"A bed that is wholly defiled, if a man dips it part by part, it is pure."[44]

---

[41]*Annot.* in Mark 7:3-4

[42]*De Emend. Templ.* L. vi. p. 771.

[43]*Hilchot. Mikvaot.* C. i. Sect. ii.

[44]*Hilchot, Celim.* C. xxvi. Sect. xiv. See also to the same purpose, IKENIUS, *Antiq. Hebraicae,* Pars i. C. xviii. & 9,

It is said that the three thousand, converted on the day of Pentecost[45] could not have been baptized by immersion the same day.

Admitting that they were all baptized the same day, which, however, is not asserted, it remains to be proved that the twelve apostles were not assisted by others. In the preceding chapter, we are informed that the number of disciples together was one hundred and twenty, among whom were doubtless many of the seventy, appointed by Christ himself. And after it is proved, that the twelve apostles were alone concerned in administering the ordinance, the expedition with which some modern baptisms of large numbers have been actually performed relieves the subject from all possible difficulty.

Another objection is thus stated: "At dead of night, in the city of Philippi, the *jailer and all his* were baptized by Paul and Silas."[46] Is it to be believed, that, in a city guarded by Roman sentinels, the *prisoners,* Paul and Silas, when their jailer had received a strict charge, at his peril, to keep them safely, would, nevertheless, take him and his family abroad, in the night, just after the whole city had been roused by an earthquake, and go to a pond, or a river, to baptize them by immersion?[47]

This case can present no difficulty to the minds of any of you, my brethren, who may have been within the yard of the prison in this city, or are acquainted with the fact, that prison yards, in the east, as well as the

---

and STACKHOUSE, *Hist. of the Bible,* B. viii. C. i. p. 1234.

[45] Acts 2:41.

[46] Acts 16:23-34.

[47] Dr. Worcester's *Letters to Dr. Baldwin.* Lett. xxii. p. 127.

yards and gardens of private houses, are usually furnished with tanks of water.

It is said again, with reference to the rites of cleansing, under the Jewish dispensation, that, "by the apostle to the Hebrews,[48] these various purifications, or *sprinklings,* are expressly called (*diaphorois baptismois*) diverse baptisms."[49]

This might be urged with some plausibility, had no immersions been prescribed in the Jewish ritual. But since these were numerous, as will appear, on examining the Levitical law,[50] the application of the word by the apostle Paul affords no reason for ascribing to it any other, beside its usual import.[51]

Another instance, supposed to be objectionable, may be thus stated. Christ promised to baptize his disciples with the Holy Spirit;[52] and on the day of Pentecost, fulfilled his promise by *pouring out* the Spirit upon them.[53] Here, it is said, the pouring out of the Spirit is

------

[48] Heb. 9:10.

[49] Dr. Worcester's *Letters to Dr. Baldwin,* Lett. xxii. p. 128.

[50] See, among other instances. Lev. 15;16:26,28; Num. 19:7-8.

[51] J. Altingius. "Washings, the Apostle calls diverse baptisms; that is, various immersions. Those Jewish washings were manifold." *Comment.* ad Heb. 9:10.

[52] Acts 1:5.

[53] Acts 2:1-4,33.

compatible with the supposition that sprinkling or pouring is baptism, but not with the supposition that immersion only is baptism.

This objection derives all its force from the erroneous supposition that the baptism of the disciples consisted in having the Spirit poured out upon them. But if the pouring out of the Spirit proves that pouring is baptism, their being filled with the Spirit proves that filling is baptism.

The truth is that the pouring out of the Spirit was merely the means by which they became baptized or immersed in the Spirit. The Spirit was poured out to such a degree that the promise of Christ was accomplished, and they were immersed, yea, filled with the Spirit. In confirmation of this interpretation, the miraculous wind (the symbol of the Holy Spirit) is represented as *filling all the house where they were sitting.*[54]

It is true, that, on this interpretation, there is no literal immersion; but since the representation is figurative, we ought not to expect a perfect resemblance in all points, but such a resemblance only as will justify the figurative application.

---

[54]Apb. TILLOTSON. *"It filled all the house.* This is that which our Saviour calls *baptizing with the Holy Ghost.* So that they, who sat in the house, were, as it were, *immersed* in the Holy Ghost, as they who were buried with water were overwhelmed, or covered all over with water, which is the proper notion of baptism." *Sermons,* Serm. cxcvii. See also, to the same purpose, Vyril, *Cateches.* xvii. & 8. 10; GURTLERUS, *Institut. Theolog. C. xxxiii;* IKENIUS, *Dissert. Philolog. Theolog.* Dissert. xix. p. 325; LE CLERC, *Remarques, sur Nouv. Test.* a Matt. 3:1; CASAUBON, in Acts 1:5; LEIGH, *Annot.* on Matt. 3:11; Bp. HOPKINS, *Works,* p. 519; Bp, REYNOLDS, *Works,* p. 226.

The same remark is applicable to the baptism of the Israelites, in the cloud, and in the sea,[55] which has been thought incompatible with the idea of immersion.

The apostle, in the context, informs us *how* they were baptized, not by being sprinkled or washed, but *by being under the cloud, and by passing through the sea.* Is there any impropriety in representing their situation, with the sea on each side, and the cloud covering them, as an immersion in the cloud, and in the sea? Is not this the natural, obvious import of the passage? As to the supposition that they were sprinkled with spray from the sea and rain from the cloud, it is made without evidence (the eighth and ninth verses of the sixty-eighth Psalm not alluding to this event[56]), and appears too fanciful, and too evidently contrived to serve a turn, to require further remark.[57]

---

[55] I Cor. 10:1-2.

[56] See Dr. Th. Scott's *Notes* on Ps. 68:9.

[57] WITSIUS. "How were the Israelites baptized in the cloud, and in the sea, seeing they were neither immersed in the sea, nor wet by the cloud? It is to be considered that the apostle here uses the term baptism in a figurative sense. The cloud hung over their heads; and so the water is over those that are baptized. The sea surrounded them on each side; and so the water in regard to those that are baptized." (*Econ. Foed.* L. iv. C. x. & 11); See also, to the same purpose, TURRETTIUNS, *Disput de Bap. Nubis et Maris*, & 24; SIR NORTON KNATCHBULL, *Animad. in Lib. Nov. Test.* ad. I Pet. 3:20-21; VENEMA, *Dissert. Sac.* L. ii. C. xiv. & 9-11; GROTIUS, in I Cor. 10:2; BRAUNIUS, *Doctrina Foed.* Loc. xviii. C. x. & 7; MR. GATAKER, *Adversar. Miscel.* Cap.

We have now considered the principal instances, in the New Testament, which have been thought to attach some other idea, beside that of immersion, to the term denoting baptism; and certainly discover no sufficient reason for departing from the etymological and established interpretation.

4. The places chosen for the administration of the ordinance, and the circumstances attending those instances, in which the act of baptizing is particularly described, in the New Testament, plainly indicate immersion.

John baptized *in the river Jordan,*[58]and in Aenon, *because there was much water there.*[59] Christ was baptized *in the Jordan,* and after the ordinance, *came up out of the water.*[60] Philip and the eunuch *went down both into the water,* and after baptism, *came up out of the water.*[61] The phrase, *went into the water,* does not, indeed, imply *in itself* that the subjects were immersed. It is one thing to go into the water; and it is another thing to be immersed. But the phrase implies *by consequence,* that the subjects were immersed. It is one thing to go into the water; and it is another thing to be immersed. For it

---

iv. CAMERO, in loc. BENGELIUS, *Gnomon,* in loc. MARCKIUS. *Bib. Exercitat.* Exod. 8 & 12; POOL'S Continuators; DR. HAMMOND and DR. WHITBY, on the place.

[58]Mark 1:5.

[59]John 3:23.

[60]Mark 1:9-10.

[61]Acts 8:38-39.

cannot be supposed that John and the primitive disciples resorted to rivers, and went into the water for the purpose of pouring or sprinkling. Do the advocates of pouring or sprinkling find this the most convenient mode of administering the ordinance?

5. Baptism is, by the apostle Paul, repeatedly compared to a burial. In one passage, believers are said, " to be buried with Christ by baptism,"[62] *and in another, "to be buried with him in baptism, and to be therein risen with him."*[63]

Whether baptism, in these passages, denotes external or spiritual baptism, it is evident that the figure derives all its propriety and beauty from some implied resemblance between the external rite and a burial; nor can it be imagined that the apostle would have ever compared baptism of any kind to a burial had there been no such resemblance.

When we are said to be spiritually circumcised, *in putting off* the body of the sins of the flesh,[64] there is an evident allusion to the nature of the external right of circumcision; and the propriety of the figure depends solely on the resemblance which can be traced between the external rite and the spiritual operation.

When Paul was exhorted to be baptized, and to *wash away* his sins,[65] there was an evident allusion to the use of water in the ordinance of baptism; and had there been no application of water on which to

---

[62]Rom. 6:4.

[63]Col. 2:12.

[64]Col. 2:11.

[65]Acts 22:16.

ground such an allusion, we may be certain that we should never have heard of washing away sins in baptism.

Accordingly, none are ever said to be washed in circumcision, because there is no resemblance between that rite and washing. So also, though we are said, in a spiritual sense, to be crucified with Christ, we are not said to be crucified with him in baptism or circumcision, because there is no resemblance between those rites and crucifixion.[66]

Nor are we ever said to be buried in circumcision, or to be risen therein to newness of life. Such expressions would be highly improper and absurd because there is nothing like a burial or a resurrection in the rite of circumcision.

---

[66]But though the apostle does not say expressly that we are crucified in baptism, does he not say this implicitly? He says that we are baptized into the death of Christ; and in the context, that we are buried with him by baptism into death, and also that our old man is crucified with him. Does he not, therefore, virtually say, that we are crucified in baptism?

It must be admitted, that, if it is good reasoning *to infer figures,* we can doubtless make out the absurdity of baptismal crucifixion. But on the same principle we can make the inspired writers answerable for the most incongruous and grotesque figures, that the wildest imagination can suggest. For instance, Christ says, I am the door, and directly after, I am the good Shepherd that giveth his life for the sheep. Shall Christ be made to say that the door gives its life for the sheep? We reply - The figure is changed, and it is not consistent with good reasoning, to infer figures, as we do literal propositions, or to reason from one figure to another.

For the same reason, we may rest assured that if baptism had consisted in sprinkling or pouring, or any partial application of water whatever, though we might possibly have heard of being washed in baptism, we should never have heard of being buried in baptism; for there being no resemblance between such applications of water and a burial, there could have been no propriety in representing baptism under such a figure.

But there is a confessed resemblance between immersion and a burial; and since the phrase, *buried in baptism,* is sanctioned by the highest authority, even divine inspiration, we have invincible proof that baptism consists not in sprinkling or pouring, but in immersion.

6. The idea of immersion is the only one, which will suit all the various connections in which the word is used in the New Testament.

The word certainly has some meaning, whether more limited, or more general; and when used to denote the ordinance of baptism, certainly has one uniform meaning, which is applicable in every instance. What is this meaning?

Is it sprinkling? We must then read, "And they were all sprinkled of him in the river Jordan."[67] Buried with him by sprinkling.[68] They were all sprinkled unto (Greek, *into*) Moses, in the cloud and in the sea.[69]

---

[67]Mark 1:5.

[68]Rom. 6:4.

[69]I Cor. 10:2.

Is it *washing*? We must then read, He shall wash you with (Greek, *in*) the Holy Ghost and fire.[70] Arise and be washed, and wash away thy sins.[71] So, many of us, as were washed into Jesus Christ, were washed into his death.[72]

The idea of immersion *always* suits the connection in which the word is used; or, in the words of Dr. Campbell, the word *"is always construed suitably to this meaning."* Thus, we may read, with propriety of sentiment and expression - And they were all immersed of him in the river Jordan, or buried with him by immersion. They were all immersed into Moses (the Mosaic religion), in the cloud and in the sea: He shall immerse you in the Holy Ghost and fire: Arise and be immersed, and wash away thy sins. So, many of us, as were immersed into Jesus Christ, were immersed into his death.

7. The Greek people certainly understand their own native language, better than any foreigners.

We must, therefore, believe that their practice, whatever it be, affords a correct and indisputable interpretation of the Greek word. Now, from the first introduction of the gospel to the present time, they have invariably practiced immersion. This is true, not only of the Greek people, but of the whole Greek church, from the southern provinces of Greece to the northern extremity of the Russian empire, a church, which,

---

[70]Matt. 3:11.

[71]Acts 22:16.

[72]Rom. 6:3

in point of territory and population, embraces nearly one half of Christendom.

DEYLINGIUS. "The Greeks retain the rite of immersion to this day, as Jeremiah, the patriarch of Constantinople, declares."[73]

MR. CHAMBERS. "In the primitive times, this ceremony was performed by immersion, as it is to this day in the oriental churches, according to the original signification of the word."[74]

DR. WALL. "All the Christians in Asia, all in Africa, and about one third part of Europe are of the last sort, (practice immersion) in which third part of Europe are comprehended the Christians of Graecia, Thracia, Servia, Bulgaris, Rascia, Wallachia, Moldavia, Russia, Nigra, and so on; and even the Muscovites, who, if coldness of the country will excuse, might plead for a dispensation, with the most reason of any...The Greek church, in all branches of it, does still use immersion; and they hardly count a child, except in case of sickness, well baptized without it."[75]

8. Not only all the branches of the Greek church, but the whole Christian world, for the space of thirteen hundred years, practiced immersion as the only real baptism.

Sprinkling or pouring was never tolerated, except in case of dangerous sickness, or want of a sufficient quantity of water, and in such cases, was called baptism by way of courtesy merely, not being regarded as real baptism, but as a substitute, which, through the indulgence of

---

[73]*De Prudent. Pastoral.* Pars. iii. C. iii. & 26.

[74]*Cyclopedia*, Art. *Baptism*, Edit. 7th.

[75]*Hist. of Inf. Bap.* Part. ii. C. ix. p. 477.

God, and (in later times) the authority of the pope, would answer the ends of baptism. Never, by any Christians, in any age, was sprinkling or pouring allowed in common cases, until the council of Ravenna, assembled by the pope, in the year 1311, declared immersion or pouring to be indifferent. From that time, the latter gradually came into general use. It was not, however, admitted into England till the middle of the sixteenth century, and not sanctioned till the middle of the seventeenth, when the Westminster assembly, influenced by Dr. Lightfoot, decided that "dipping of the person in water, is not necessary; but baptism is rightly administered, by pouring or sprinkling water upon the person."[76]

As the truth of these assertions concerning the practice of the church must be established by testimony, independently of argumentation, I hope to be excused for the number and length of the following quotations from Paedobaptist authors of acknowledged authority.

GROTIUS. "That baptism used to be performed by immersion, and not by pouring, appears both from the proper signification of the word, and the places chosen for the administration of the rite, John 3:23; Acts 8:38; and also from the many allusions of the apostles, which cannot be referred to sprinkling, Rom. 6:3-4; Col. 2:12."[77]

VITRINGA. "The act of baptizing is the immersion of believers in water. This expresses the force of the word. Thus also it was performed by Christ and the apostles."[78]

---

[76]*Confession*, Chap. xxviii. 3.

[77]Apud Poli *Synops.* ad Matt. 3:6.

[78]*Aphorismi Sanct. Theolog.* Aph. 884.

CURCELLOEUS. "Baptism was performed by plunging the whole body into water, and not by sprinkling a few drops, as is now the practice. Nor did the disciples, that were sent out by Christ, administer baptism afterwards, *in any other way.*"[79]

WESTMINSTER ASSEMBLY OF DIVINES. "*Buried with him by baptism.* See Col. 2:12. In this phrase, the apostle seems to allude to the ancient manner of baptism, which was to dip the parties baptized, and, as it were, to bury them under the water."[80]

CALVIN. "From these words, John 3:23, it may be inferred, that baptism was administered by John and Christ, by plunging the whole body under water. Here we perceive how baptism was administered among the ancients; for they immersed the whole body in water."[81]

BAILEY. "Baptism, in strictness of speech, is that kind of ablution or washing, which consists in dipping; and when applied to the Christian institution, so called, it was used by the primitive Christians, *in no other sense than that of dipping,* as the learned Grotius and Casaubon well observe."[82]

---

[79]*Relig. Christ. Institut.* L. V. C. ii.

[80]*Annot.* on Rom. 6:4. See also, to the same purpose, Bp. PEARCE, *Note* on I Cor. 15:29; and Bp. BURNET, *Expos.* xxxix. *Articles*, p. 374.

[81]In John 3:23. *Comment.* in Acts. 8:38.

[82]*Dictionary*, Dr. Scott's Edit. 1772.

DR. WALL.[83] "We should not know by these accounts," (John 3:23; Mark 1:5; Acts 8:38) whether the whole body of the baptized was put under water, head and all, were it not for two later proofs, which seem to me to put it out of the question. One, that St. Paul does twice, in an allusive way of speaking, call baptism a burial, which allusion is not so proper, if we conceive them to have gone into the water, only up to the armpits, as it is, if their whole body was immersed. The other, the custom of the near succeeding times. As for sprinkling, I say, as Mr. Blake, at its first coming up in England, *Let them defend it that use it.*"[84]

BINGHAM. "There are a great many passages in the epistle of St. Paul which plainly refer to this custom (immersion), 'As this was *the original apostolical practice; so it continued to be the universal practice of the church, for many ages,* upon the same symbolical reasons as it was first used by the apostles. It appears from Epiphanius and others, that almost all heretics who retained any baptism retained immersion also. The only heretics against whom this charge (of not baptizing by a *total* immersion) is brought, were the Eunomians, a branch of the Arians.'"[85]

DR. TOWERSON. "But, therefore, as there is so much the more reason to represent the rite of immersion as *the only legitimate rite* of

---

[83]In a general convocation of the English clergy, Feb. 9, 1706, it was ordered, "that the thanks of this house be given to Mr. Wall, vicar of Shoreham in Kent, for the learned and excellent book he hath lately written, concerning infant baptism." In Dr. Baldwin's *Bap. of Believers only*, Part. ii. Sect. iv. p. 91.

[84]*Def. of Hist. of Inf. Bap.* p. 131, 140.

[85]*Origines Eccles.* B. xi. C. xi.

baptism, because it is *the only one* that can answer the ends of its institution, and those things which were to be signified by it; so especially, if (*as is well known, and undoubtedly of great force*) the general practice of the primitive church was agreeable thereto, and the practice of the Greek church, to this very day. For who can think, either the one, or the other, would have been so tenacious of so troublesome a rite, were it not, that they were well assured, as they of the primitive church might very well be, of its being *the only instituted and legitimate one?*"[86]

VENEMA. "It is without controversy, that baptism, in the primitive church, was administered by immersion into water, and not by sprinkling. The essential act of baptizing, in the second century, consisted, not in sprinkling, but in immersion into water, in the name of each person in the Trinity. Concerning immersion, the words and phrases that are used, sufficiently testify; and that it was performed in a river, a pool, or a fountain. To the essential rite of baptism, in the third century, pertained immersion, and not aspersion, except in cases of necessity, *and it was accounted a half-perfect baptism.* Immersion, in the fourth century, was one of those acts that were considered as essential to baptism: - nevertheless, aspersion was used in the last moments of life, on such as were called clinics, and also, where there was not a sufficient quantity of water."[87]

SALMASIUS. "The ancients did not baptize, otherwise than by immersion, either once or thrice; except clinics, or persons confined to their beds, who were baptized in a manner of which they were capable; not in the entire laver, as those who plunge the head under water; but the

---

[86] *Of the Sacram. of Bap.* Part. iii. p. 58.

[87] *Hist. Eccles.* Secul. i. & 138; Secul. ii. & 100; Secul. iii. & 51; Secul. iv. & 110.

whole body had water poured upon it (Cypr. iv. Epist. vii.). Thus, Novatian, when sick, received baptism, being *perichutheis (sprinkled),* not *baptistheis (baptized).* Euseb. vi. *Hist.* C. xliii."[88]

Bp. TAYLOR. "The custom of the ancient churches was not sprinkling, but immersion; in pursuance of the sense of the word (baptize) in the commandment, and the example of our blessed Savior. Now this was of so sacred account in their esteem, that they did not account it lawful to receive him into the clergy who had been only sprinkled in his baptism, as we learn from the epistle of Cornelius to Fabius of Antioch, *apud. Euseb.* L. vi. C. xliii. It was a formal and solemn question, made by Magnus to Cyprian, whether they are to be esteemed right Christians, who were only sprinkled with water, and not washed or dipped."[89]

CYPRIAN. (*In reply to Magnus.*) "You ask, dear son, what I think of those, who, in sickness, receive the sacred ordinance; whether, since they are not washed (loti) in the saving water, but have it poured on them, (perfusi), they are to be esteemed right Christians.[90] In the saving sacraments, when necessity obliges, and God grants his indulgence,

---

[88] Apud Witsii (*Econ. Foed.* L. iv. C. xvi. & 13.

[89] *Ductor Dubitantium,* B. iii.C. iv. Rule 15.

[90] It cannot be disputed what kind of washing Cyprian intends, for none suppose that baptism has ever been performed in any other way than by immersion, and pouring or sprinkling.

abridgments of divine things (divina compendia), will confer the whole on believers."[91]

DR. WALL. "Anno Dom. 215, Novatian was, by one party of the clergy and people of Rome, chosen bishop of that church, in a schismatical way, and in opposition to Cornelius, who had been before chosen by the major part, and was already ordained. Cornelius does, in a letter to Fabius, Bishop of Antioch, vindicate his right, and shows that Novatian came not canonically to his orders of priesthood, much less was he capable of being chosen bishop; for that all the clergy, and a great many of the laity, were against his being ordained presbyter, because it was not lawful, they said, for any one that has been baptized in his bed, in time of sickness (*ton en kline dia nosan perichuthenta*), as he had been, to be admitted to any office of the clergy."[92]

CORNELIUS. "He (Novatian) fell into a grievous distemper, and it being supposed that he would die immediately, he received baptism, being sprinkled with water on the bed whereon he lay, *if that can be termed baptism.*"[93]

VALESIUS. "As sick persons who were baptized in their beds, could not be immersed by the priest, they had only water poured on them (perfundebantur). Therefore, this kind of baptism was accounted informal and imperfect; for it appeared to be received, not voluntarily, but through fear of death, by men laboring under distraction of mind, and actuated by no suitable views; *and since baptism properly signifies immersion, this kind of affusion could scarcely be called baptism.* Wherefore, clinics

---

[91]*Epistola ad Magnum*, Edit. Paris, 1643.

[92]*Hist. of Inf. Bap.* Part. ii. C. ix. p. 463.

[93]*Epist. ad Fabium*, apud Euseb. *Hist. Eccles.* L. vi. C. xliii.

(for so they were called, who received this kind of baptism) were, by the twelfth canon of the council of Neocaesarea, prohibited from the priesthood."

THE MONKS OF CRESSY. "Is it lawful, in case of necessity, occasioned by sickness, to baptize an infant, by pouring water on its head, from a cup, or the hands?"[94]

POPE STEPHEN III *(In reply to the monks of Cressy).* "Such a baptism, performed in such a case of necessity, shall be accounted valid."[95]

BASNAGE. "This (the response of Stephen, in the year 754) is accounted the first law against immersion. The pontiff, however, did not dispense with immersion, except in case of extreme necessity. This law, therefore, did not change the mode of dipping, in public baptisms; and it was not till five hundred and fifty seven years after, that the legislature,

---

[94]*Annot.* in Euseb. *Hist. Eccles.* L. vi. C. Xliii. p. 120. Hence it appears, that the validity of clinic baptism was disputed, not only because the sincerity of the recipients was questionable, but because they had not been immersed. Such also was the opinion of Bp. Taylor, (see above,) and Dr. Cave, *Prim. Christ.* P. i. C. x. p. 196. The same appears from the words of Cornelius to Fabius, and still clearer from the reply of Cyprian to Magnus, which evidently implies that the objection of his correspondent was founded, not on any supposed deficiency in the recipient, but on the imperfection of the rite itself.

[95]Apud Labbei, *Concilia,* Tom. vi. p. 1650

in a council at Ravenna, in the year 1311, declared immersion and pouring indifferent."[96]

VENEMA. "Beveridge, on the fiftieth apostolical canon, asserts, that the ceremony of sprinkling began to be used instead of immersion, about the time of Pope Gregory, in the sixth century; but without producing any testimony in favor of his assertion; and it is undoubtedly a mistake. Martene declares in his *Antiq. Eccles. Rit.* L. i. P. i. C. i. that in all the ritual books, or pontifical manuscripts, ancient or modern, that he had seen, immersion was required; except by the Cenomanensian, and that of a more modern date, in which pouring on the head is mentioned. In the council of Ravenna, also, held in the year 1311, both immersion and pouring, if a vessel could not be had; therefore, only in case of necessity."[97]

DR. WHITBY. "It being so expressly declared here (Rom. vi. 4) and Col. ii. 12, that we are *buried with Christ in baptism,* by being buried under water, and the argument to oblige us to a conformity to his death, by dying to sin, being taken hence; *and this immersion being religiously observed by all Christians for thirteen centuries,* and approved by our church (of England) and the change of it into sprinkling, even without any allowance from the Author of this institution, or any license from any council of the church, being that which the Romanist still urgeth to justify his refusal of the cup to the laity; it were to be wished that this custom might

---

[96]*Monumenta,* Vol. i. Pradfat. C. v. & 4, in Robinson's *Hist. of Bap.* C. xxxiii.

[97]*Hist. Eccles.* Secul. vi. & 251.

be again of general use, and aspersion only permitted, as of old, in case of the *clinici*, or in present danger of death."[98]

STACKHOUSE. "Accordingly, several authors have shown, that we read no where in scripture of any one's being baptized but by immersion; and from the acts of councils, and ancient rituals, have proved, that this manner of immersion continued, as much as possible, to be used, for *thirteen hundred years* after Christ."[99]

DR. WALL. "France seems to have been the first country in the world, where baptism by affusion was used ordinarily to persons in health, and in the public way of administering it. It being allowed to weak children (in the reign of Queen Elizabeth) to be baptized by aspersion, many fond ladies and gentlewomen first, and then, by degrees, the common people, would obtain the favor of the priest, to have their children pass for weak children, too tender to endure dipping in the water. As for sprinkling, properly called, it seems it was at 1645, just then beginning, and used by very few. It must have begun in the disorderly times after 1641. They, the assembly of divines in Westminster, reformed the font into a basin. This learned assembly could not remember, that fonts to baptize in had been always used by the primitive Christians, long before the beginning of popery, and ever since churches were built; but that sprinkling, for the common use of baptizing, was really introduced (in France first, and then in other popish countries) in times of popery: *And that, accordingly, all those countries, in which the usurped power of the pope is, or has formerly been owned, have left off dipping of children in the font; but that all other countries in the world, which had never regarded*

---

[98]*Note* on Rom. 6:4.

[99]*Hist of the Bible*, B. viii. C. i.

his authority, do still use it; and that basins, except in cases of necessity, were never used by papists, or any other Christians whosoever, till by themselves."[100]

"The way that is now ordinarily used, *we cannot deny to have been a novelty*, brought into this church, by those that had learned it in Germany, or at Geneva. And they were not contented to follow the example of pouring a quantity of water (which had there been introduced instead of immersion) but improved it, if I may so abuse that word, from pouring to sprinkling; that it might have as little resemblance of the ancient way of baptizing as possible."[101]

Let me conclude this part of the discourse with one remark. The question which we have examined, evidently relates, not to the *mode*, but the *nature* of baptism. We have not been inquiring, *how baptism must be performed, in order to be valid*; but simply, *what baptism is*. If the several considerations which have been presented are sufficient to show that baptism is immersion, it is equally clear that the terms, *baptism* and *immersion*, are equivalent and interchangeable, and that when Christ commanded his disciples to be baptized, he commanded them to be immersed.

---

[100]*Hist. of Inf. Bap.* P. ii. C. ix.

[101]*Def. of Hist. of Inf. Bap.* p. 403.

Part II
To Whom Is Baptism
to Be Administered?

The words of the great commission are, *Go ye, therefore, and teach* (or rather *disciple*) *all nations, baptizing them into (eis) the name of the Father, and of the Son, and of the Holy Ghost.* Is there any difficulty in understanding these plain instructions? Did not Christ obviously intend, that the apostles should make disciples among all nations, and then baptize them? He surely did not intend that they should baptize whole nations indiscriminately; but those of the nations who should become disciples.[102] This is confirmed by the terms of the commission, as recorded by

---

[102]DR. CAMPBELL. *"Go, therefore, convert all the nations, baptizing them, &c.* There are manifestly three things which our Lord here distinctly enjoins his apostles to execute, with regard to the nations: to wit (*mathatenein*), (*baptizein*), (*didaskein*), that is, to convert them to the faith, to initiate the converts into the church by baptism, and to instruct the baptized in all the duties of a Christian life." *Four Gospels,* and *Note,* on the place.

    MR. BAXTER. *"Go, disciple me all nations, baptizing them.* As for those that say they are discipled by baptizing,. and not before baptizing, they speak not the sense of that text. When Christ layeth down, in the apostolical commission, the nature and order of his apostles' work, it is first to make disciples, and then to baptize them into the name of the Father," &c. *Disputat. of right to Sacram.* p. 91, &c.

another evangelist: "Go ye into all the world, and preach the gospel to every creature. *He that believeth, and is baptized,* shall be saved."[103]

Notwithstanding the obvious import of the law of baptism, the greater part of the Christian world baptize the children of believers, on the faith of their parents, or the profession of their sponsors, and refuse baptism to believers, if they have been baptized in infancy. Does their practice appear consistent with the command of Christ? Christ commands those who believe, to be baptized. Paedobaptists adopt a system, which tends to preclude the baptism of believers. They baptize the involuntary infant, and deprive him of the privilege of ever professing his faith in the appointed way. If this system were universally adopted, it would banish believers' baptism out of the world. But leaving the evident discordance between the system of Paedobaptists and the command of Christ, let us inquire whether infant baptism has any just support, either direct or inferential.

When any practice is proposed and enforced as a binding duty, we have a right to examine the grounds of the alleged obligation. It is not sufficient for the proposer to show that the practice is innocent, and even compatible with every other duty: it is requisite that he prove it binding. If one should enforce the ancient custom of dressing in white, for several days after baptism, as the duty of every Christian, it would not be necessary for us to urge one argument against it; nor would it be sufficient for him to prove it innocent, and even compatible with every other duty. We might reasonably refuse compliance until he should prove, that we are bound to comply. So, in the case of infant baptism, it is not necessary for us to urge one argument against it; nor is it sufficient for the proposer to prove that every objection is groundless. It is requisite for him to prove that it is obligatory. The question with every parent

---

[103]Mark 16:15-16.

ought to be, Am I under obligation to have my children baptized? Now, on what grounds is this obligation predicted?

We should naturally expect that the baptism of infants, if enjoined at all, would have been enjoined in the law which instituted the ordinance of Christian baptism. But this law is silent on the subject of infants. Has not Christ, however, left some other command, enjoining infant baptism? Not one. Have not the apostles, who were intrusted with farther communications of the will of Christ, left some command on this subject? Not one. Have they not left us some example of infant baptism? Not one. Have they not spoken of baptized infants, and thus given undeniable intimation of this practice? No, in no instance. On the contrary, whenever they have spoken of baptism, or of those to whom it was administered, their language implies that baptism was a voluntary act of worship, and the baptized, professing believers. "As many of you," said Paul to the Galatians, "as have been baptized into Christ, *have put on Christ*."[104]

But does not the baptism of the *households* of Lydia, the jailer, and Stephanas afford some evidence in favor of this practice? As the term *household* does not necessarily imply infants, these instances, though admitted without examination, cannot be considered as furnishing any certain precedent in favor of the baptism of infants. Do they afford any presumptive evidence?

It appears, that Lydia was a woman of Thyatira, residing in Philippi, for the purpose of trade.[105] It does not appear, that she had a husband or children. It is more probable that her household was composed of assistants in her business, who, following her example,

---

[104]Gal. 3:27.

[105]Acts 16:14-15.

believed and were baptized. For we are informed that when Paul and Silas left the city, they entered into the house of Lydia and saw and comforted *the brethren.*[106]

In the case of the jailer,[107] Paul and Silas "spake unto him the word of the Lord, and *to all that were in his house.*" And he "rejoiced, believing in God, *with all his house.*"[108] Concerning the household of Stephanas, Paul writes, at the close of the epistle, [109] "That it is the first-fruits of Achaia, and *that they have addicted themselves to the ministry of the saints.*"[110]

---

[106]Acts 16:40.

[107]Acts 16:23-34.

[108]DR. MACKNIGHT. *"Having believed in God with all his house;* who, it seems, were equally impressed with Paul's sermon, as the jailer himself was." *Life of the Apostle Paul,* Chap. 5.

CALVIN. "In which also the grace of God illustriously appeared, because it suddenly brought the whole family to a pious consent." *Comment.* in loc.

[109]I Cor. 16:15.

[110]DR. MACKNIGHT. "The family of Stephanas seem all to have been adults when they were baptized. For they are said, chap. 16:15, *to have devoted themselves to the ministry to the saints.*" *Translation of the Apost. Epist.* Note 1st. on I Cor. 1:16.

DR. GUYSE. "It therefore seems - that the family of Stephanas were all adult believers, and so were baptized

Thus, in each of these instances, especially in the two latter, some circumstances appear which lead us to conclude that the members of these households were professing believers. It may, therefore, be repeated *that there is no precept nor precedent in scripture for infant baptism.* Let us next examine the inferential evidence, adduced in favor of this practice.[III]

---

upon their own personal profession of faith in Christ." *Note* on I Cor. 1:16.

[III]It must be evident, that, in the above, I do not object to infant baptism, "because it is not enjoined by any express command." The sum of my objection is this - there is no command - there is no example - there is no inferential evidence. I do indeed believe that a New Testament command or example is the only proper ground, on which any Christian ordinance can be supported; and that is incorrect to reason from a positive institute under one dispensation to a positive institute under another. But many cannot see the correctness of this distinction; and as I wish to accommodate myself to all capacities, I place the subject on open ground, and say - prove it directly, or prove it inferentially - only prove it.

But suppose we should say that express precept or example is requisite to support any ordinance. What then? Why, they exclaim, where is your express command for female communion? Where, for baptizing "adults born of Christian parents?" and (why not add?) where, for baptizing a man over fifty years old, or for baptizing Burmans and Hindoos? The pertinence of such objections may be illustrated by a case (See Watts' *Essays* Glasgow, p. 71).

A master orders his servants to mark the fruit trees

in a certain field. The first proceeds according to orders. The second proceeds to mark other than fruit trees. Stay, says the first, none but fruit trees. Our master has expressly ordered fruit trees to be marked, and in my opinion, we are to mark no trees but such as are expressed in the order. Indeed, says the second - then leave this orange and yonder pomegranate, for they are not expressly mentioned in the order. But, replies the first, since we are ordered to mark fruit trees, all trees of that description, whether orange or pomegranate, olive or tamarind, being expressed by the generic term *fruit trees*, are expressly ordered to be marked.

Thus when believers are commanded to be baptized, all persons who sustain this character, whether born of Christian parents or not, whether men or women, of whatever age and whatever country, being expressed by the generic term *believers*, are expressly commanded to be baptized.

Thus, also, when church members, saints, and all who in every place, call on the name of Jesus, are commanded to partake of the Lord's supper (I Cor. 1:2, and 11:17-34), and when instances are recorded in which the disciples, those who received the word and were baptized, did partake (Acts 20:7 and 2:41-42). all persons who sustain these characters, whether men or women, old or young, bond or free, being expressed by the generic terms *believers, disciples, church members,* &c. are expressly commanded to partake of the Lord's supper.

But where is your express command for women? We have no express command for women, as such, or for men, as such, or for children, as such; but we have an express command for believers; and if this man, that

1. Children, it is said, have been connected with their parents in covenant with God, and, in consequence of this connection, have received, by divine appointment, the initiating seal; their covenant connection has never been dissolved, nor their right to the initiating seal disannulled.[112]

It does not follow that children are connected with their parents in every covenant because they were connected with their parents in one covenant. The whole strength of the argument now presented rests in the supposition that the covenant of grace, in which Christians now stand, is the same with the covenant of circumcision, in which children were connected with their parents. The latter covenant is recorded in the seventeenth chapter of Genesis.

"And when Abram was ninety years old and nine, the Lord appeared to Abram, and said unto him, I am the Almighty God; walk before me, and be thou perfect. And I will make my covenant between me and thee, and will multiply thee exceedingly. And Abram fell on his face; and God talked with him saying, As for me, behold my covenant is with thee, and thou shalt be a father of many nations. Neither shall thy name any more be called Abram, but thy name shall be called Abraham; for a father of many nations have I made thee. And I will make thee exceedingly fruitful, and I will make nations of thee, and kings shall come out of thee. And I will establish my covenant between me and thee, and thy seed after thee in their generations, for an everlasting covenant, to be a God unto

---

woman, and yonder child, are believers, we have an express command for them in the character of believers.

[112]See Dr. WORCESTER'S *Letters to Dr. Baldwin*, Let. xxi. p. iii.

thee, and to thy seed after thee. And I will give unto thee, and to thy seed after thee, the land wherein thou art a stranger, all the land of Canaan, for an everlasting possession; and I will be their God. And God said unto Abraham, Thou shalt keep my covenant, therefore, thou, and thy seed after thee, in their generations. This is my covenant, which ye shall keep, between me and you and thy seed after thee: Every man child among you shall be circumcised. And ye shall circumcise the flesh of your foreskin: and it shall be a token of the covenant betwixt me and you. And he that is eight days old shall be circumcised among you, every man child in your generations, he that is born in the house, or bought with money of any stranger, which is not of thy seed. He that is born in thy house, and he that is bought with thy money, must needs be circumcised; and my covenant shall be in your flesh, for an everlasting covenant. And the uncircumcised man child, whose flesh of his foreskin is not circumcised, that soul shall be cut off from his people; he hath broken my covenant." The covenant proceeds, with regard to Sarah and Ishmael, and closes in the twenty-second verse.

I now ask the Christian parent, Is this the covenant which God has made with you? Has God covenanted to give you *these* blessings? Though he may have covenanted to give you some of these blessings, together with many others, the question must be repeated, *Is this the very covenant which God has made with you?* If, on examining the several parts of the covenant, you feel authorized to answer in the affirmative, I reply, You are under sacred obligation to perform your part. You are under sacred obligation to circumcise, or (if you are satisfied that baptism is substituted) to baptize "every man child - that is eight days old:" It is in direct disobedience of the command of God to baptize before the eighth day, or to defer baptism beyond the eighth day. It is an entire departure from the command of God to baptize a female child, or to withhold baptism from one "that is born in the house, or bought with money of any stranger, which is not of thy seed." God has, in no part of his word, released you from your obligation to baptize *on the eighth day*. Nor has he required you to baptize a female child. "Who hath required this at your hand?" Nor has he released you from your obligation to baptize the servant, born in the house, or bought with money.[113]

---

[113]Gal. 3:28. *There is neither Jew nor Greek, there is neither bond nor free, there is neither male nor female; for ye are all one in Christ Jesus.* This passage has been produced both as a declaration of the right of female infants to baptism, and as a repeal of the right of servants.

It is important, in construing scripture, to adopt the very meaning which the inspired writer obviously intended to convey; and not to suffer the mind to lay hold on some distant meaning, which is contrary to the whole scope of the context, and probably would never have occurred, had not an hypothesis needed its support. If the latter licentious mode of interpretation be tolerated, any doctrine, however trifling or contradictory, any practice, however puerile or pernicious, may be proved to be scriptural.

In the passage before us, let us ascertain what characters are described, and in what respect they are one in Christ Jesus.

Ver. 26. *For ye are all the children of God, by faith in Christ Jesus.* 27. *For as many of you, as have been baptized into Christ, have put on Christ.* 28. *There is neither Jew nor Greek, there is neither bond nor free, there is neither male nor female; for ye are all one in Christ Jesus.* Is it not too evident to require any remark, that the apostle is speaking of believers only, such as are the children of God by faith in Christ, and have put on Christ

But I ask again, Do you really believe that God has promised you the very blessings which he promised Abraham and his seed? Do you really believe that God has promised to give you the land of Canaan, *even that land, in which your father Abraham was a stranger?* If not, whatever blessings God has promised to give you, whatever covenant he has made with you, it is not *the* covenant which he made with Abraham, and in which children were connected with parents.

That the promise of the land of Canaan was, at least, one principal promise in the covenant of circumcision, appears from the numerous passages in which it is distinguished and presented as the substance of the covenant. God said to Moses, "I appeared unto Abraham, unto Issac, and unto Jacob - and I have also established my covenant with them, *to give them the land of Canaan, the land of their pilgrimage, wherein they were strangers.*"[114]David exhorted Israel; "O ye seed of Israel, his servant, ye children of Jacob, his chosen ones - Be ye mindful always of

---

by being baptized?

The Galatians, through the influence of Judaizing teachers, had imbibed the error that, in order to be justified, it was necessary to be circumcised, and to keep the Mosaic law. The chief object of the apostle, in this epistle, and particularly in this chapter, is to show that we must be justified by faith alone; that it is not necessary to become a Jew in order to be justified; for in Christ Jesus, no distinction of nation, outward condition, or sex, is of any avail. In Christ Jesus, there is neither Jew nor Greek, bond nor free, male nor female. *If ye have faith in Christ, whatever be your descent or condition, ye are all on an equality, in point of acceptance with God.*

[114]Exod. 6:3-4

his covenant; the word which he commanded to a thousand generations; even of the covenant which he made with Abraham, and of his oath unto Isaac; and hath confirmed the same to Jacob for a law, and to Israel for an everlasting covenant, saying, *Unto thee will I give the land of Canaan, the lot of your inheritance.*"[115] The same sentiment prevailed in the time of Nehemiah; for on a day of fasting, the whole congregation of Israel addressed God in prayer: "Thou art the Lord the God, who didst choose Abram - and madest a covenant with him, *to give the land of the Canaanites - to his seed.*"[116]

The covenant of grace does not contain this promise. When we contemplate two covenants, and see that one principal article, contained in the one, is not contained in the other, by what singular process can the mind be brought to the conclusion that these two covenants, so palpably different and distinct, are one and the same? But is it urged that "the covenant made with Abraham, is expressly declared to be an everlasting or perpetual covenant; a covenant to continue to the latest generation."[117] And was not the land of Canaan given to Abraham and his seed, for an *"everlasting* possession?" Even when the covenant is represented as "the word, which God commanded *to a thousand generations,*" the promise of the land of Canaan is brought forward as the chief thing, yea, as the very sum and substance of this everlasting covenant.

So also the priesthood was confirmed to Phinehas and *his seed* in an *everlasting* covenant.[118] So also the feast of expiation, on the tenth day

---

[115] I Chron. 16:13-18

[116] Neh. 9:7-8

[117] DR. WORCESTER'S *Two Discourses*, Disc. I. p. 27

[118] Num. 25:13

of the seventh month, was established by a statute, which was declared to be an *everlasting* statute.[119] It is urged that the covenant "comprised all the blessings and privileges ever promised to believers and the church." Whether this be true or not, since it comprised one blessing, which is not comprised in the covenant of grace, it cannot be the same covenant. But is it true?

The two principal promises made to the seed of Abraham are, that God would give them the land of Canaan, and that he would be their God. What is the import of the latter promise? Is there any absurdity in saying that God was the God, not only of the few pious descendants of Abraham, but of the nation of Israel at large? Was he not the God of the Jews, in a sense in which he was not the God of the Gentiles? Did he not select the posterity of Abraham, in the line of Isaac and Jacob, and distinguish them above all other nations? Did he not protect them from their enemies, and grant them a rich abundance of temporal blessings? Did he not give them his law, and establish among them his worship, and the ordinances of his house? Did he not, by these spiritual advantages, furnish them with opportunities which no other nation enjoyed, of obtaining him as their spiritual portion? Is there any absurdity in saying, that, in these respects, he was the God of the nation at large? If not, is there any absurdity in supposing that his promise imported that he would be their God in these respects?

God is represented, in the scriptures, as the God of his people, in different senses. When, in the new covenant, he promises to put his laws in their minds, and to write them in their hearts, and to be to them a God,[120] the promised renewal of heart shows that the latter promise

---

[119] Lev. 16:34

[120] Heb. 8:10

imports that he will be the *spiritual* portion of his people. When, in the Revelation, it is promised that God will be with men, and be their God,[121] the connection shows that the promise imports that he will be their *eternal* portion. When, in the covenant of circumcision, he promised to be the God of the seed of Abraham, the connection of this promise with other promises, and the manner of fulfillment, show that the promise imported that he would multiply and protect them; that he would grant them an abundance of temporal blessings; and that he would distinguish them above all other nations by spiritual advantages.

The seed to which the land of Canaan was promised was most evidently the lineal descendants of Abraham. To the same seed the Lord promised to be a God. Mark the terms of the promises: "I will give unto thee, and to thy seed after thee, the land wherein thou art a stranger, all the land of Canaan for an everlasting possession; and I will be *their* God." But he was not their God, in a spiritual sense. It appears from their history, that, in every age, a remnant only were truly pious.

Those who maintain that he promised to be the spiritual portion of the seed of Abraham are obliged to explain the promise to mean that God would be the God of *some* of the seed of Abraham. Is this a fair explanation? Is it not using undue freedom with the word of God? Is it not indeed frittering away the plain import of scripture?

Suppose that a king should promise peculiar privileges to a faithful subject and his posterity; not *all* or *some*, but simply, his posterity. Would not the subject be authorized to expect that all his posterity would enjoy these privileges? Suppose that it should appear that the king actually conferred certain peculiar privileges on all the posterity, excepting those who refused his kindness. Suppose further, that it should appear that the king had selected from among his subjects a number, in

---

[121]Rev. 21:3

which were some of the posterity of the faithful subject, and raised them to nobility. Would there be any doubt concerning the import of the king's promise to his faithful subject? Could it be urged, with any appearance of probability, that when he promised peculiar privileges to the posterity of this subject, he did not intend those which he actually conferred on a very few of them?

God covenanted to give the land of Canaan and his favor to the posterity of Abraham, in the line of Isaac. That his posterity were not to come into immediate possession of the land had been previously stipulated.[122]God faithfully performed his promises. He conferred the blessings promised on the posterity of Abraham, in the line of Isaac, excepting those only who rejected his kindness. A refusal to accept a promised favor always releases the promiser from his obligation, unless (is it necessary to add?) the promised favor includes such a disposition of the heart as precludes refusal. Esau and his posterity, as well as many of the posterity of Jacob, refused to accept the Lord as their God; not merely as their spiritual portion, but as their God in the sense promised. They acknowledged and worshipped other gods. The Israelites frequently forsook God; and he as frequently forsook them. But when they repented and returned to him, he remembered his covenant, and delivered them from their distresses. At length, they rejected him in the most decided manner, by rejecting his Son. They would not have him to reign over them. Since that time God has forsaken them. But when they shall repent and return, God will again remember his covenant. The manner, however, in which he will restore his favor, though intimated in the prophecies, can be learned from the event only.

What is the ground taken by the advocates of the covenant of circumcision? Do they say that God promised to be the God of

---

[122]Gen. 15:13-16

Abraham's seed, in a spiritual sense, *if they accepted the promise?* "This would be a complete abandonment of their argument. For it would place such as claim interest in the covenant of circumcision exactly upon a level with all others. God has engaged to save all who reverence, worship and obey him, though Abraham be ignorant of them, and Israel acknowledge them not."

Do they say that the promise imported, "that, *on condition of faith and fidelity on Abraham's part, in respect to his children*, they should become subjects of grace, and heirs of the blessings of the covenant."[123] But have we a right to make conditions which God has not made? Have we a right to take his covenant, and fashion it to suit our preconceived, favorite sentiments? God did not promise, I will be a God to thy seed, on condition of faith and fidelity on thy part, in respect to thy seed. Neither in this covenant, nor in any of his communications with Abraham, did God inform him that the grand condition on which he would be a God to his seed, was *fidelity on his part, in respect to his seed.*[124]

---

[123]DR. WORCESTER'S *Two Discourses*, Disc. I, p. 36

[124]Gen. 18:19, *For I know him, that he will command his children, and his household after him; and they shall keep the way of the Lord, to do justice and judgment; that the Lord may bring upon Abraham that which he hath spoken of him.* Much stress has been laid on the auxiliary *shall*, as implying an engagement to the family of Abraham, in consequence of his fidelity in instructing them. In the original, the grammatical construction of the verb *smr* rendered *they shall keep*, is precisely of the same import as the grammatical construction of the preceding verb *swh*, rendered *he will command*. No reason, therefore, can be given, why the verbs should not be constructed similarly in the translation. For the same reason that the preceding verb

But it is said, that in this covenant, God required Abraham *to walk before him, and to be perfect.* Is this a condition of the covenant? Did God suspend the performance of his promises on the perfection of Abraham? Surely, then, this was not the covenant of grace. Under the new dispensation we are indeed commanded to love God with all our heart, and to be perfect in holiness. God requires this of all mankind, under every dispensation. It would be derogatory to his character to require less. But this is not a *condition* of the covenant of grace. The blessings of the covenant are not suspended on such a condition. If we are interested in Christ by faith, notwithstanding our imperfections and sins, God will be our God *through grace.* Yet the author above cited, says, "To become entitled to the blessings of the covenant, Abraham must walk before God, and be perfect."[125] If so, this covenant was certainly not the covenant of grace. It might be expected, therefore, that the advocates of this covenant would, for the sake of their own cause, readily admit, and strenuously maintain what appears to be the fact, that this requirement was not a condition of the covenant, or even a part of the covenant, but merely a preamble or introduction to the covenant. God introduces the solemn transaction by saying, *Walk before me, and be thou perfect.* Then follows, *I will*

---

is rendered *will command,* ought the following to be rendered *will keep.* This passage appears to contain a prediction, rather than an engagement. God foresaw that Abraham would be faithful in instructing his family; that they would observe the requirements taught them; and that, with a view to this obedience, both on the part of Abraham and his family, it would be suitable for him to bestow on them the promised blessings.

[125] Dr. Worcester's *Two Discourses,* Disc. I, p. 34.

make my covenant with thee. Then are presented the terms of the covenant; first, the part which God would perform, consisting in the bestowment of several blessings on Abraham and his seed; and secondly, the part which Abraham and his seed were to perform, consisting in the observance of the rite of circumcision; and lastly, several explanatory and restricting articles, with regard to Sarah and Ishmael and Isaac. That the observance of the rite of circumcision was, emphatically, *the* condition of this covenant, appears from the manner in which it is presented, the conspicuous place which it holds in the covenant, and the penalty attached to its neglect. "And the uncircumcised man child - shall be cut off from his people; *he hath broken my covenant.*"

It is a popular and prevailing sentiment that this promise imports that so many of the seed shall be subjects of grace, that the church shall be perpetuated *"in the line of natural descent."* Is this hypothesis consistent with facts? Has not God transferred the church from the posterity of Abraham to the Gentiles? Is it said that the Jews were rejected because of unbelief? But has not God the hearts of all in his hand? And had he not, on this hypotheses, promised that the church should be perpetuated in the posterity of Abraham? Why, then, did he not perform? But this is not the only transfer. If the Christian church is the same with the Jewish, and if the same promises are made to the former as were made to the latter, may it not be asked, Where are the descendants of the once flourishing churches in the north of Africa? Where are the descendants of all the Asiatic churches, planted by the apostles themselves? They are now covered with the darkness of Mahomedan superstition. Surely, we are not there to look for the Church of Christ. This church is now transferred to the west of Europe, and embraces the descendants of those who were bowing down to idols of wood and stone during the prosperity of the eastern churches.

It is true that God regards the prayers of pious parents for their offspring, and frequently grants his blessing on their religious instructions. We may, therefore, expect that in places where the truth has prevailed, a pious seed will be preserved for some generations. But that this is God's uniform mode of operation, or that he has covenanted to perpetuate the church, *in the line of natural descent,* a slight glance at ecclesiastical history must effectually disprove.

Let us next consider several passages in the New Testament, in which it has been supposed that the covenant of circumcision is recognized as the covenant of grace. On the day of Pentecost, Peter addressed the Jews: "The promise is unto you, and to your children, and to all that are afar off, even as many as the Lord our God shall call."[126] The expression, *unto you and to your children,* resembling the expression *unto thee and to thy seed,* used in the covenant of circumcision, has occasioned the supposition that this is a repetition of one of the promises contained in that covenant. There were several promises made to Abraham and his seed. Does the context lead us to suppose that Peter intended one, rather than another? Or was one of the promises called by way of eminence, *the* promise? Is it probable that Peter alluded to one of the promises in this covenant, calling it *the* promise, when, through his whole discourse, he had not spoken of Abraham, or of any covenant made with him? Is it not probable - is it not certain, that he alluded to the promise concerning which he had been discoursing from the first?

The Jews were astonished at the pouring out of the Spirit on the disciples. Peter states the event as a fulfillment of the promise spoken by the prophet Joel: "And it shall come to pass, in the last days, saith God,

---

[126]Acts 2:39.

I will pour out my Spirit upon all flesh; and *your sons and your daughters shall prophesy,*" &c.[127]

In the progress of this discourse, he says that Jesus, having received of the Father *the promise of the Holy Ghost,* hath shed forth this; and finally, he exhorts them, "Repent and be baptized every one of you, in the name of Jesus Christ, for the remission of sins, and ye shall receive *the gift of the Holy Ghost. For the promise is unto you, and to your children,* and to all that are afar off, even as many as the Lord our God shall call." More summarily, thus; God said, I will pour out my Spirit upon all flesh, even on your sons and daughters: Jesus hath received this promise, and begun to perform it, by shedding forth this on us, his disciples; repent ye, therefore, and ye shall receive the same gift; the Spirit shall be poured out on you; for the same promise is made to you and your children, &c.[128]

In the epistle to the Galatians, it is written, "If ye be Christ's, then are ye Abraham's seed, and heirs according to the promise."[129] Let us inquire, what is implied in believers being the seed of Abraham; and what promise is here intended. In the context (ver. 6, 7) it is written, "Even as Abraham believed God, and it was accounted to him for

---

[127]Ver. 17.

[128]In this explanation of the promise, I am happy to agree with WITSIUS, *Exercitat. in Symb.* Exercit. xi & 19; LIMBORCH, *Comment.* in loc. VENEMA, *Dissertat. Sac.* L. iii. C. iv. & 7, 8; Dr. OWEN, *Doct. of Saints' Perseverance,* p. 116; Dr. HAMMOND, *Works,* Vol i. p. 490; Dr. WHITBY, *Annot.* on the place; and Dr. DODDRIDGE, *Note,* on the place.

[129]Gal. 3:29.

righteousness: Know ye, therefore, that they which are of faith, the same are the children of Abraham." Abraham believed; therefore, they who believe are his children. This is perfectly in the style of scripture. The unbelieving Jews are called children of the devil, because they were like the devil in their character and conduct. On the same principle, the profligate are called children of Belial; believers, children of light; and unbelievers, children of disobedience. On the same principle, believers are called children of Abraham. They are like Abraham in character and conduct. They have the faith of Abraham.

But why are they called children of Abraham, rather than of some other patriarch, or holy man of old, whose faith they likewise imitate? The reason is most obvious. The apostle addressed this and most of his epistles to churches composed of converted Jews and persons imbued with Jewish sentiments - persons who constantly heard from the Jews, with whom they consorted, of the high privilege of being descended from Abraham. Most pertinently, therefore, does he exhort them: Be not bewitched, ye foolish men, with such representations. If ye have the faith of Abraham, whether descended from him or not, ye are really his children to every valuable purpose, being his spiritual seed; for if ye resemble Abraham in his faith, rest assured that ye will resemble him in his reward; your faith, like his, will be accounted for righteousness. And thus, as the natural seed are heirs of the land of Canaan and the temporal blessings secured in the covenant of circumcision, ye, the spiritual seed, are heirs of the far more excellent, the spiritual blessings, secured in the covenant of grace. For "if children, then heirs." Accordingly, the apostle continues, "And the scripture, foreseeing that God would justify the heathen through faith, preached before the gospel unto Abraham, saying, *In thee shall all nations be blessed.* So then, they which be of faith are blessed with faithful Abraham." And again (ver.14) "That the blessing of Abraham might come on the Gentiles, through Jesus Christ." And in the last verse, "And if ye be Christ's, then are ye Abraham's seed, and heirs according to the promise."

There can be no doubt that the blessing, of which believers are heirs, is justification by faith; and that the promise, according to which they are heirs of this blessing, is the *gospel promise* made to Abraham. The apostle's reasoning may be summarily stated thus: As Abraham was justified by having his faith accounted for righteousness; and as the blessing of Abraham is come on the Gentiles, through Jesus Christ, so that they who are of faith are blessed with faithful Abraham, according to the promise, In thee shall all nations be blessed; ye, believing Gentiles, being, by faith, the children of Abraham, are, according to the promise, heirs of the blessing of justification by faith.[130]

---

[130]Dr. MACKNIGHT, on Gal. 3:16. *Translation.* "Now to Abraham were the promises spoken, and to his seed. (See ver. 19.) He doth not say, And in seeds, as concerning many, but as concerning one person, And in thy seed, who is Christ."

Note. He does not say, And in seeds. So *tois spermas* should be translated, the preposition *en* being understood here, as is plain from the promise itself, Gen. 22:18. *And in thy seed shall all the nations of the earth be blessed.* (See Acts 3:25; also *Luther's Commentary on Galatians*, p. 308.) The apostle having affirmed, ver. 15, that, according to the customs of men, none but the parties themselves can set aside or alter a covenant that is ratified, he observes in this verse that the promises in the covenant with Abraham were made to him and to his seed. The promise to Abraham is that recorded Gen. 12:3. *In thee shall all the families,* LXX. *Pasai ai phulai,* all the tribes, *of the earth be blessed.* The promise to his seed is that recorded Gen. 22:18. *And in thy seed shall all the nations of*

The same sentiments are contained in the epistle to the Romans: "For we say that faith was reckoned to Abraham for righteousness. How was it then reckoned? When he was in circumcision, or in uncircumcision? Not in circumcision, but in uncircumcision. And he

---

the earth be blessed. See ver. 19. Now since by the oath which God swore to Abraham, after he had laid Isaac on the altar, both promises were ratified, the apostle reasons justly when he affirms, that both promises must be fulfilled. And having shown, ver. 9, that the promise to Abraham to bless all the families of the earth in him means their being blessed as Abraham had been, not with justification through the law of Moses, as the Jews affirmed, but with justification by faith, he proceeds, in this passage, to consider the promise made to Abraham's seed, that in it likewise all the nations of the earth should be blessed. And from the words of the promise, which are not, *in thy seeds,* but *in thy seed,* he argues that the seed in which the nations of the earth should be blessed is not Abraham's seed in general, but one of his seed in particular, namely, Christ, who, by dying for all nations, hath delivered them from the curse of the law, that the blessing of justification by faith might come on believers of all nations, through Christ, as was promised to Abraham and to Christ.

Dr.GUYSE. "The covenant that I have given a hint of (ver 8, 9, 14,) relating to the way of our being accepted of God as righteous, consisted of a free promise, which, because of its vast comprehension of blessings, and of its being first made to Abraham, and afterwards repeated to him, and to Isaac (Gen. 12:3, and 22:18, and 26:4), may be called *the promises.*" *Paraphrase* on Gal. 3:16.

received the sign of circumcision, a seal of the righteousness of the faith, which he had, yet being uncircumcised: that he might be the father of all them that believe, though they be not circumcised: that righteousness might be imputed unto them also."[131] *He received the sign of circumcision, a seal of the righteousness of the faith, which he had, yet being uncircumcised.* The meaning of the apostle cannot be that Abraham performed circumcision on himself and family, and thus *sealed his faith,* or attested his faith, as believers seal or attest their faith by solemn acts of worship. Not his faith, but the righteousness of his faith, was sealed. Man may seal or attest his faith by acts of worship and obedience; none but God can seal the righteousness of faith. None but God can declare faith imputable for righteousness. Abraham received the sign of circumcision as a divine attestation of the righteousness of his faith; or, in the words of Stephen, "God gave him the covenant of circumcision,"[132] and thus sealed the righteousness of his faith, or declared that his faith was accounted for righteousness. Still further, God attested the righteousness of that faith which Abraham had *in uncircumcision,* and thus established him the father of all them that believe, though they be not circumcised, that righteousness might be imputed to them also. Had not the righteousness of *this* faith been attested, it might have been doubted whether Abraham was the father of any but circumcised believers, in such a sense as that they would be heirs of his blessing, or have their faith imputed for righteousness. But God attested the righteousness of that faith, which he had in uncircumcision, and thus proved, that it is not so much circumcision, as faith, that makes us children of Abraham; and consequently (for if children, then heirs) that, if we have his faith, though we be not circumcised, our faith, like

---

[131]Rom. 4:9-11.

[132]Acts 7:8.

his, will be imputed for righteousness, and thus we become heirs of the blessing of justification by faith, according to the promise made to Abraham, In thee shall all nations be blessed.

This gospel promise, an ever memorable charter of all the blessings which Jewish and Gentile believers enjoy through Christ, is not contained in the covenant of circumcision, but in a covenant made with Abraham, at the time of his calling, twenty-four years before, and recorded in the twelfth chapter of Genesis.[133] This covenant was confirmed to Abraham, by an oath, when he offered up Isaac;[134] "that by two immutable things," a promise and an oath, "in which it was impossible for God to lie, we might have a strong consolation."[135] This covenant was renewed to Isaac and Jacob, together with the covenant of circumcision.[136] This is the covenant which the apostle Peter, "on the bright morning of the gospel day," presented in these words: "Ye are the children of the prophets, and of the covenant, which God made with our fathers, saying unto Abraham, *And in thy seed shall all the kindred's of the earth be blessed.*"[137] This is the covenant, which being "confirmed before of God in Christ, the law, which was four hundred and thirty years after," and we

---

[133] Ver. 2-3.

[134] Gen. 22:16-18.

[135] Heb. 6:18.

[136] Gen. 26:3-4 and 28:13-14.

[137] Acts 3:25.

may add, the covenant of circumcision, which was twenty-four years after, "cannot disannul, that it should make the promise of none effect."[138]

But it will be said that in the fourth of Romans we find an incontestable application of one of the promises in the covenant of circumcision. The apostle represents Abraham's being the father of believers as a fulfillment of the promise that he should be a father of many nations.[139] The New Testament writers frequently apply historical and prophetical passages of the Old Testament in a secondary sense, without giving any intimation of their primary import. The Lord said by the prophet Hosea, "When Israel was a child, then I loved him, and called my son out of Egypt."[140] This is applied by an evangelist to the return of Jesus from Egypt, without any intimation of its primary import.[141] The Jews were commanded not to break a bone of the paschal lamb.[142] This is applied by another evangelist, directly to Jesus, without any intimation of its primary import.[143] In the case before us, God constituted Abraham a father of many nations. This is applied, by an apostle, to Abraham's being the father of all believers, without any intimation of its primary import and fulfillment.

---

[138]Gal. 3:17.

[139]Ver. 17.

[140]Hos. 11:1.

[141]Matt. 2:15.

[142]Exod. 12:46.

[143]John 19:36.

These instances illustrate the principle, on which the New Testament frequently proceeds, in applying events and predictions recorded in the Old Testament. We are to use their application with proper caution. We are not to extend the parallel between the type and the antitype further than we are authorized by the inspired penman.

When the evangelist represents the return of Jesus from Egypt, as a fulfillment of that which was spoken by the Lord; "Out of Egypt have I called my son," he recognizes some kind of identity between Jesus and the people of Israel. When the apostle represents the relation between believers and Abraham as a fulfillment of that which was spoken to Abraham, "A father of many nations have I made thee," he recognizes some kind of identity between the posterity of Abraham and believers. In both cases, the recognition of identity is of the same kind, and to the same extent. But we do not infer from the former application that Jesus and Israel are the same in any other respect than that they both are sons of God, though in very different senses, and were both called out of Egypt. Nor from the latter are we to infer that believers and the posterity of Abraham are the same in any other respect than that they both have Abraham for a father, though in very different senses; the one, on account of natural descent, the other, on account of faith. We instantly discover the impropriety of extending the parallel between Israel and Jesus, or of reasoning from the former to the latter. And is it not as evidently improper to extend the parallel between the posterity of Abraham and believers? Or to infer that the latter are under the same covenant as the former?

Though the evangelist John presents the fact that the soldiers broke not the legs of Christ as a fulfillment of the prophecy, implied in the command respecting the paschal lamb, "Neither shall ye break a bone thereof," and thus, in the most unequivocal manner, recognizes an identity between the paschal lamb and Christ, yet we do not hesitate to infer that the lamb was merely a type of Christ. And we do not feel authorized to reason from the type to the antitype. We do not conclude that Christ is subject to the same rules of treatment as the paschal lamb; or that those who partake of Christ are bound by the Mosaic ritual to use the same ceremonies as the Jews in partaking of the paschal lamb. Yet this may be proved, by the same kind of reasoning as it can be proved from the allusion of the apostle under consideration, that believers are subject to the same regulations, or are in the same covenant, as the posterity of Abraham. But in the words of Dr. Scott, when speaking of another instance of "forging figurative language into a literal meaning, and so grounding doctrines upon it, - common sense is usually sufficient to preserve men from such absurdities, when there is no personal or party interest to serve by them."[144]

Let me now call your attention to the important fact that, with regard to the Gentiles, the token of the covenant of circumcision has been forbidden. When certain Jews from Jerusalem taught the believing Gentiles at Antioch that, except they were circumcised after the manner of Moses, they could not be saved, the council of Apostles and elders, assembled in Jerusalem under the special direction of the Holy Spirit, wrote and concluded that the brethren "observe no such thing."[145] Accordingly, Paul wrote to the Corinthians, "Is any man called in uncircumcision, let him not be circumcised;"[146] and to the Galatians,

---

[144]*Note* on I Cor. 10:4.

[145]Acts 15:1-31 and 21:25.

[146]I Cor. 7:18.

"Behold, I Paul say unto you, that if ye be circumcised, Christ shall profit you nothing."[147]

2. Is not the prohibition of the token of a covenant an explicit declaration that the covenant is abolished?

God instituted the rite of circumcision to be the token of a certain covenant, which he made with Abraham and his seed, and declared, at the same time, that he who did not receive the token had broken the covenant. Such a token is one species of language. Wherever it appears, it conveys an idea of what it was instituted to represent. The language of the rainbow is, there will never again be a deluge. The language of the sign of circumcision is, such a covenant exists between the seed of Abraham and God. After this language has been allowed for several centuries, to the natural and also to the adopted seed, it is finally, with regard to the Gentiles, expressly forbidden. God says, let this language be no longer used; let it be no longer said, that such a covenant exists between me and any Gentile.

It is urged that, though the rite of circumcision is abolished, the rite of baptism is substituted as a token of the same import. But if this be true, should we not expect to find baptism enjoined when circumcision is forbidden? Should we not expect to find this substitution clearly stated in scripture? Yet, in no instance where circumcision is forbidden is there any intimation of baptism. Nor is this substitution mentioned in any passage, through the whole of the New Testament. It is not mentioned, or even intimated, in those instances, where, had it been really made, the circumstances render the omission perfectly unaccountable. Notwithstanding the Judaizing teachers greatly complained that

---

[147]Gal. 5:2.

circumcision was not enforced on the Gentiles, the substitution of baptism, which would have furnished a complete answer, was never suggested by the apostles. Notwithstanding the Galatians had imbibed a belief of the necessity of circumcision, and Paul wrote an epistle expressly to correct their mistake, yet, throughout this epistle, no distant intimation is given of the very thing which must have completely satisfied their minds, and silenced all opposition.

On the contrary, so far were the Jewish converts from believing in this substitution, that even after they were commanded to be baptized themselves, though already circumcised, they continued, under the direction of the apostles, to circumcise their children. The elders at Jerusalem said to Paul, The Jews that are zealous of the law, "are informed of thee, that thou teachest all the Jews, which are among the Gentiles, to forsake Moses, saying, that they ought not to circumcise their children, neither to walk after the customs. Do, therefore, this that we say to thee, - *that all may know, that those things, whereof they are informed concerning thee, are nothing.*"[148]

But as the substitution of baptism in the place of circumcision is generally considered absolutely essential to the Paedobaptist cause, you will naturally presume, that though the scripture is silent on the subject, and though facts recorded in scripture are adverse to the supposition, still something plausible can be urged in its favor. Let me, therefore, present to your view, accompanied with a few remarks, the four arguments which a late distinguished writer has advanced in proof of this substitution.[149]

---

[148]Acts 21:20-24

[149]Dr. WORCESTER'S *Letters to Dr. Baldwin*, Let. xvi.

A. "Baptism is now, as circumcision anciently was, an instituted pre-requisite to a regular standing in the visible church."

Not to question the propriety of calling the Jewish and Christian churches collectively the visible church, it is sufficient here to observe that circumcision was not pre-requisite to a regular standing in the church; otherwise, females were not regular members.

B. "Baptism, under the present dispensation, is of the same significance with circumcision under the ancient. As circumcision signified the renovation of the heart, or regeneration; so baptism signifies the same thing."

But did circumcision, as it was commanded to be administered among the Jews, signify that the subject was regenerated? Surely not. In all languages, terms which literally denote sensible objects are sometimes figuratively used to convey ideas of immaterial or spiritual objects. But we do not infer that the former objects are signs of the latter. The term *heart,* which literally denotes a part of the body, is figuratively used to denote the affections of the mind. But we do not infer that the former is a sign of the latter. Circumcision, in the literal acceptation, separated the Jews from the Gentile world, and brought them into a state of relative holiness. Hence, the term was figuratively used to signify moral separation from the world, and real holiness of heart. But it is preposterous to infer, from this figurative use of the word, that circumcision signified regeneration.

Admitting, however, that circumcision and baptism are both significant of regeneration, it does not follow that *the general significance* of the two ordinances is the same because there is a similarity of significance in one particular. Circumcision chiefly signified that the subject was interested in that covenant which God made with Abraham, and of which he expressly declared this ordinance to be the token. Baptism is represented as an act of worship, by which the baptized profess the religion of Christ, and signify their fellowship with Christ, in death and resurrection, and their being washed from sin. How different the leading import of the two ordinances.

C. *"Baptism, under the present dispensation, is a seal of the same thing of which circumcision was a seal under the ancient. We have the express declaration of the apostle that circumcision was a seal of the righteousness of faith. - Of the same righteousness of faith, baptism is now also a seal."*

God gave Abraham the sign of circumcision, and thus sealed the righteousness of the faith which he had in uncircumcision. But the *performance* of this rite, though it might seal or attest the faith of an adult subject, could not attest the righteousness of his faith; much less could it attest the righteousness of their faith, who never exercised any faith. That the *administration* of baptism can attest the righteousness of faith is equally impossible. And that baptism is an attestation from God of the righteousness of faith, has been scarcely advanced, much less proved.

D. *"That baptism is come in the place of circumcision, we are decisively taught, by the apostle, in Col. 2:10-13. 'And ye are complete in him, which is the head of all principality and power. In whom also ye are circumcised, with the circumcision made without hands, in putting off the body of the sins of the flesh, by the circumcision of Christ; buried with him in baptism, wherein also ye are risen with him, through the faith of the operation of God, who hath raised him from the dead. And you, being dead in your sins, and the uncircumcision of your flesh, hath he quickened together with him.'"*

In this passage, we are taught that the Colossians were spiritually circumcised in putting off the body of the sins of the flesh, and spiritually baptized by being buried with Christ, and being raised to newness of life.[150]Thus they are represented as having passed the whole process of death, burial and resurrection. The death, the putting off the body, is called circumcision, in allusion to the nature of that rite; and the burial and resurrection are fitly represented in the ordinance of baptism or immersion. But though some other explanation of the passage should be adopted, is it possible, since the apostle is speaking of *spiritual* circumcision and spiritual baptism, both of which have been received by the Colossians, to make out an inference that external baptism has come in the place of external circumcision?

A view of these *four arguments* may serve to convince you of how little can be said in support of a point, which, on account of its importance in the Paedobaptist system, demands the fairest and most invincible proof; and may lead you to adopt the sentiment contained in the following words of Dr. Emmons: "Can we justly conclude that it is the duty to circumcise them? The truth is, we must learn the peculiar duties of believers under the present dispensation of the covenant of grace, from the dispensation itself, *which enjoins all the peculiar duties which belong it.*"[151]

3. By many Paedobaptist writers, especially the advocates of national churches, the argument from the Abrahamic or Jewish dispensation is stated in a manner somewhat different from that which we have been considering.

---

[150]See Rom. 6:4.

[151]*Dissert. on the Qualifications for the Christian Sacraments*, Chap. ii. Sect. v.

Infants, they say, *were constituted members of the visible church; they have never been excluded from the church, and consequently are now members.* This argument, when analyzed, stands thus: Infants were constituted members of the Abrahamic or Jewish church; they were never excluded from this church; therefore they are members of the Christian church. Is this conclusive? The whole strength of the argument rests in the supposition that the Christian church is the same with the Abrahamic or Jewish. How can this be proved?

It cannot be proved by showing that they are founded on the same covenant; for there is no evidence that the covenant of circumcision is the same with the covenant of grace.

Nor can it be proved, by adducing promises and prophecies of the perpetuity of Zion and her final triumph and glory. Some of these promises and prophecies relate to the final conversion and restoration of the Jewish people. Others evidently belong to the true church; to that Zion that includes all the saints who existed before the organization of a visible church, and all the truly pious, whether they have belonged to any organized visible church or not. No one denied the perpetuity and identity of the church of God, to which the promises and prophecies belong. In order to make the application of these promises and prophecies bear on the subject, it is necessary to show that they belong not to that church which commenced in the persons of our first parents, and will continue to the end of the world, but to a particular organized body, which commenced in the family of Abraham.

Nor can the point be proved from the apostle's discourse concerning the olive tree, from which the Jews, the natural branches, were broken off, and into which the believing Gentiles were engrafted;[152] unless it be shown that the olive tree represents that particular organized body,

---

[152]Rom. 11:16-24.

the Abrahamic or Jewish church, or in the words of Dr. Austin, "the society of Israel."

It is evident that the olive tree cannot represent this body or society as existing under the Sinai law, for Gentile believers are not introduced into a similar state. And is it not equally evident, that, for a similar reason, it cannot represent this body or society as founded on the covenant of circumcision? The engrafted branches are represented as partaking of the root and fatness of the olive tree. But whatever blessings Gentile believers enjoy, they do not enjoy the peculiar blessings secured in the covenant of circumcision. They do not inherit the land of Canaan, though that was one distinct, principal promise in this covenant. Nor can it be admitted that they enjoy the favor of God, in that sense, and in that only, in which it was engaged to the posterity of Abraham.[153] The olive tree cannot, therefore, represent the community of Israel, as founded on

---

[153]Dr. AUSTIN. "The reinsertion of these broken off branches into the good olive tree (alluding to the restoration of the Jews) 'can mean no less than their occupying the place which they held before they were broken off. Occupying this place, they necessarily partake of the fatness of the olive tree. This is the blessing, the entire blessing secured in the promise. But the land of Canaan is expressly a part of this blessing. Their being brought back then under the covenant must necessarily restore them to the enjoyment of this land.'" *View of the Economy of the Church of God*, Chap. xiv. p. 305.

If this reasoning be correct, it follows that Gentile believers cannot be considered as engrafted into the olive tree, because they do not inherit the land of Canaan, which is expressly a part of the blessing secured in the promise, and represented by the fatness of the olive.

the covenant of circumcision; nor, for the same reason, can it represent the covenant itself.

Christ said to his disciples, "I am the true vine, and my Father is the husbandman. *Every branch in me that beareth not fruit, he taketh away.*"[154]This may suggest the proper interpretation of the symbolical language of the apostle. The olive tree may represent the Messiah, as presented in the gospel promise made to Abraham and in subsequent promises, in which all the pious cordially rested, and in which the Jews, *as a nation,* professed to rest. They are called natural branches, conformably to the language of the evangelist, "He came unto *his own,* and *his own* received him not."[155]The natural branches were unfruitful, and, therefore, according to the prediction of Christ, were taken away; or, in the style of the apostle, because of unbelief they were broken off; and in their place the believing Gentiles were engrafted, and now partake of the root and fatness of the olive tree, the riches of grace in Jesus Christ.

Nor can it be proved that the churches are the same by showing that they are alike in some respects. Much labor has been expended in exhibiting those points in which the churches are alike. But surely, two things may be alike in many respects, and still not be the same. It is granted that they are not alike in all respects. The very point, therefore, necessary to be proved, is, that they are alike in that respect which concerns the question, the mode of introduction, or the requisites to admission. To ascertain whether two institutions are alike in any one respect, we must form an idea of each, from all the information we can obtain, and compare the ideas.

---

[154]John 15:1-2.

[155]John 1:11.

On examining the Scriptures with regard to the Jewish church, we find that it was *a select race,* composed chiefly of the posterity of Abraham in the line of Isaac and Jacob. To be descended from Abraham, in this line, was sufficient to introduce the subject into the Jewish church. Persons of Gentile extraction, also, who were purchased by Jews, or wished to enjoy the privileges of Jews, could be introduced into this church by circumcision.[156] Whether any other requisite to admission was appointed by God, we are not informed. This church continued nearly two thousand years. At length, Christ came, and according to ancient prophecies, *set up his kingdom* in the world.[157] He abolished the distinction which had so long subsisted between the posterity of Abraham and other nations, and either in person, or by his Spirit, selected his followers from both Jews and Gentiles, thus making "in himself, *of twain, one new man.*"[158]

On examining the Scriptures, with regard to this new kingdom, the Christian church, we learn, from the formation of particular churches, and the instructions addressed to the members, as well as from addresses made to both Jews and Gentiles who were without, that it is a society, composed of *select individuals,* who, not merely collectively or nationally, but personally, profess faith in Christ: credible evidence of personal piety being the requisite to admission. Whether natural descent, or any religious rite is sufficient to introduce the subject into this church, we are not informed. We have, therefore, no evidence, that, in that respect, which concerns the question before us, the two churches are alike.

---

[156] Exod. 12:44-49.

[157] Dan. 2:44.

[158] Eph. 2:15.

It has, however, been supposed that the church membership of infants is supported in the following passage: "Suffer little children, and forbid them not, to come unto me; *for of such is the kingdom of heaven.*"[159] In the Gospels of Mark and Luke, it follows, "Whosoever shall not receive the kingdom of God, as a little child, he shall not enter therein."[160] We cannot suppose that our Lord used words, in such different senses, in the same speech, as would unavoidably mislead his hearers. In the latter passage, the kingdom of God denotes heaven, and to receive the kingdom, as a little child, is to receive it with the humility and docile disposition which characterize children. This passage explains the former. Of such, says Christ, is the kingdom of heaven. Does he mean, of such in age and size, of such in the moral temper of the heart, or of such in humility and docility of disposition? His subsequent remark determines in favor of the latter meaning. Nor is this a singular application of the phrase. On another occasion, he says, "Except ye be converted and become as little children, ye shall not enter into the kingdom of heaven."[161] He certainly does not mean, Except ye become as little children, in age and size, but in humility; for he immediately adds, "Whosoever, therefore, shall *humble himself, as this little child,*" &c.[162]

---

[159] Matt. 19:14.

[160] Mark 10:15 and Luke 18:17.

[161] Matt. 18:3.

[162] Matt. *Suffer little children.* Mark. *Suffer* the *little children.* Luke. *Suffer little children.* It should, however, be observed, that, in the original, the expression is the same in each gospel. The article is uniformly inserted; though, by our translators, it is omitted in the Gospels of Matthew and

The following passage also has been supposed to favor the church membership of infants: "For the unbelieving husband is sanctified by the wife, and the unbelieving wife is sanctified by the husband; *else were your children unclean; but now are they holy.*"[163] The holiness ascribed to the children cannot be moral holiness, for it is ascribed to the unbelieving parent also. Nor can it be ceremonial or federal holiness, securing a title to church membership, or any church privilege; for though it is ascribed to the unbelieving parent, he is not considered a member of the church, or entitled to any church privilege. Nor is this interpretation consistent with the apostle's reasoning. It appears that the Corinthians have inquired of the apostle, whether it was lawful for believers, who were married to unbelievers, to continue the marriage connection. The apostle determines that it is lawful; for, says he, the unbeliever is sanctified by the believer, that is, as "every creature of God is good, and nothing to be refused, if it be received with thanksgiving; for it is *sanctified* by the word of God and prayer."[164] In this sense, the unbeliever is sanctified, so that it is lawful for the parties to dwell together. Now if it was not lawful to dwell together, your children would, of consequence, be unclean. But they are not unclean. Therefore, you may be satisfied that your cohabitation is lawful marriage. But to urge the church membership of children, or their title to

---

Luke. Without the article, the words of Christ seem to form a *general* direction concerning little children; but, with the article, they evidently form a *particular* direction, concerning *those children*, whose approach the disciples were preventing.

[163] I Cor. 7:14.

[164] I Tim. 4:4-5.

any church privilege, as proof that the unbeliever is sanctified to the believer, so that it is lawful for them to dwell together, would have been quite irrelevant.[165]

The question returns, is there any evidence that the Jewish and Christian churches are the same? Or that the children of believers are members of the Christian church, as the children of Jews were members of the Jewish church? We cannot believe without evidence. And clear evidence is requisite to support a sentiment, which counteracts the first impressions we receive from the word of God; still clearer, to support a sentiment fraught with consequences embarrassing and dangerous.

Are we ready to acknowledge the children of believers as members of the Christian church, in the same sense as the children of Jews were members of the Jewish church? Are we ready to acknowledge their right to the Lord's supper, as soon, at least, as they are capable of discerning the Lord's body? And the consequent obligation of the church, to require their attendance, and to discipline them, if they neglect to attend? To

---

[165] The interpretation here adopted is strengthened by the use of the word *hagiasmos*, in I Thes. 4:3, 4, 7, and approved by AMBROSE, who says, "The children are holy, because they are born of lawful marriage," MUSCULUS and MELANCTHON, in Tombe's *Exercitation*, p. 11, 12, 13; CAMERARIUS, VATABLUS and CAMERO, in loc. VELTHUYSIUS, *Opera*, Tom. i. p. 801; SUARES and VASQUES, apud Chamieri *Panstrat.* Tom. iv. L. v. C. x. & 50; DIETERICUS, apud Wolfi *Curae*, in loc. See also Dr MACKNIGHT, who says, "I, therefore, think with Elsner, that the words in this verse have neither a federal nor a moral meaning, but are used in the idiom of the Hebrews," &c. *Translation of the Apost. Epist.* Note on I Cor. 7:14.

consider and treat them as members of the church, until formally excluded; and to consider and treat them as not members, until formally admitted, are very different things. The latter is the uniform practice of Protestant dissenters in England and their descendants, the churches in America; the former only is consistent with the principle that the children of believers are church members. But it most evidently tends to confound the church with the world, and, it is to be feared, is the most pernicious practice that ever infested and laid waste the vineyard of the Lord.

4. An attempt has been sometimes made to support the practice of infant baptism on the ground of the Jewish proselyte baptism. The argument is this. The Jews were in the habit of receiving proselytes, both adults and infants, by baptism, as well as by circumcision. Christ and his apostles being acquainted with this practice when he commanded them, in general terms, *to teach all nations, baptizing them, he must have intended, and they must have understood him to intend, that baptism to which they had been accustomed, the baptism of infants as well as adults.*

This argument would have some force, were there any sufficient evidence that the Jews, in the time of Christ, or in any preceding age, admitted proselytes by baptism. But there is not the slightest evidence of Jewish proselyte baptism in the Old Testament, or in the New, and therefore, no sufficient evidence; for if we admit "the perfection of scripture, as a Christian's only rule of faith and practice," we cannot imagine that we are left to discover the truth of a doctrine, as we sometimes are, the meaning of an original word from uninspired writings; we cannot imagine, with Dr. Wall and others, that proselyte baptism, of which there is no trace in the word of God, is the proper ground on which to support infant baptism. It may, however, afford satisfaction to the minds of some, to be further assured that there is no intimation of proselyte baptism in the apocryphal writings, or in the works of Philo and

Josephus, who both wrote concerning the laws and customs of the Jews, or in any other ecclesiastical writings about the time of Christ, or in the Targums or Chaldee Paraphrases, or in the works of the Christian fathers, for the first three or four centuries. The first mention of proselyte baptism is in the Jewish Talmuds, which were composed between the second and fifth centuries; and the manner in which it is mentioned in the Talmuds, shows that it was then a novel and questionable practice. Accordingly, though some learned Paedobaptists, in their zeal to find some foundation for infant baptism, have suffered themselves to be imposed on by the Jewish rabbins, others have the candor to express themselves in the following manner:

Dr. JENNINGS. "But after all, it remains to be proved, not only that Christian baptism was instituted in the room of proselyte baptism, but that the Jews had any such baptism in our Saviour's time. The earliest accounts we have of it are in the Mishna and Gemara; the former compiled, as the Jews assert, by Rabbi Juda, in the second century; though learned men, in general, bring it several centuries lower; the latter, not till the seventh century. There is not a word of it in Philo, nor yet in Josephus, though he gives an account of the proselyting of the Idumeans by Hyrcanus."[166]

Dr. OWEN. "The institution of the rite of baptism is no where mentioned in the Old Testament. There is no example of it in those ancient records; nor was it ever used in the admission of proselytes while the Jewish church continues. No mention of it occurs in Philo, in Josephus, in Jesus, the son of Sirach, nor in the Evangelical History. This Rabbinical opinion, therefore, owes its rise to the Tanneroe, or Ante-Mishnical doctors, after the destruction of their city. The opinion of some learned men, therefore, about the transferring of a Jewish baptismal

---

[166]*Jewish Antiq.* Vol. I. p. 136.

rite (which in reality did not then exist) by the Lord Jesus, for the use of his disciples, *is destitute of all probability.*"[167]

Dr. LADNER. "As for the baptism of Jewish proselytes, I take it to be a *mere fiction of the Rabbins,* by whom we have suffered ourselves to be imposed upon."[168]

Provided that the command of Christ to teach did not limit his subsequent command to such as were taught, it is, doubtless, fair reasoning, that when Christ, in general terms, commanded his apostles to baptize, he must have intended, and they must have understood him to intend, that kind of baptism to which they had been accustomed. So far the argument would be good. But there is no sufficient evidence that the baptism to which they had been accustomed was proselyte baptism of adults and infants. To what kind of baptism, then, had they been accustomed? We know of none but the baptism of John. But John did not baptize infants. His baptism was a baptism of repentance, and acknowledgment of Him that was to come, and, therefore, a baptism of adults only. This was the baptism which the disciples of Jesus administered, in the beginning of his ministry, as it is written, "that Jesus made *and baptized more disciples* than John; though Jesus himself baptized not, but his disciples."[169] The baptism of adults was that to which alone they had been accustomed; and therefore, if Christ, in general terms,

---

[167]*Theologoumena,* L. v. Digress, iv.

[168]*Letters to and from Dr. Doddridge,* Let lxxxix. p. 275. But for a full examination of the subject, see Dr. GILL'S *Dissertation concerning the Baptism of Jewish proselytes.*

[169]John 4:1-2.

commanded his apostles to baptize, he must have intended, and they must have understood him to intend, the baptism of adults only.

5. The following quotations present to our view the last ground to which Paedobaptists resort.

BOSSUET. "Experience has shown; that all the attempts of the Reformed to confound the Anabaptists, by the scripture, have been weak; and, therefore, *they are, at last, obliged to allege to them the practice of the church.*"[170]

CHAMBERS. "As none but adults are capable of believing, they (the German Baptists) argued that no others are capable of baptism; especially, as there is no passage, in all the New Testament, where the baptism of infants is clearly enjoined. Calvin, and other writers against them, are pretty much embarrassed to answer this argument; and *are obliged to have recourse to tradition, and the practice of the primitive church.*"[171]

Also the *Oxford Divines,* in a convocation, held one thousand, six hundred and forty-seven, acknowledged, "that, without the consentaneous judgment of the universal church, they should be at a loss, when they are called upon for proof, in the point of infant baptism."[172]

What, then, is the evidence from antiquity, in favor of infant baptism? It has been already stated that the writers of the New Testament are silent on this subject, whether recording the formation of the primitive churches, or addressing epistles to those churches. They

---

[170]In Stennet's *Answer to Russen,* p. 184.

[171]*Cyclopedia.* Art. *Anabaptists.*

[172]In Lawson's *Baptismalogia,* p. 116.

frequently mention the baptism of believers; but preserve a profound silence on the baptism of infants.

The Christian writers of the first century who immediately succeeded the apostles - Barnabas, Hermas, Clemens Romanus, Ignatius, and Polycarp - usually called, by way of distinction, *apostolical fathers*, frequently mention the baptism of believers; but, like the inspired penmen, are entirely silent on the subject of infant baptism.

The Christian writers of the second century - Justin Martyr, Athenagoras, Theophilus of Antioch, Tatian, Irenaeus, and Clemens Alexandrinus - frequently mention the baptism of believers; but, like the inspired penmen and the apostolical fathers, never mention infant baptism.

There is, indeed, in the writings of Irenaeus, one passage which has been adduced in proof of this practice: "Christ passed through all the ages of man, that he might save all by himself, that is, all who, by him, are regenerated to God, infants, and little ones, and children, and youths, and persons advanced in age."[173]

As the word translated *regenerated*, sometimes in the writings of the Christian fathers denotes *baptism*, some have supposed, that, in this passage, it may be properly translated *baptized*. The passage would then stand, Christ came to save all by himself - that is, *all who, by him, are baptized to God,* &c.

There are two considerations which forbid this translation. First: It makes the passage unintelligible. It is intelligible that all who are saved are *regenerated* by Christ; but what possible meaning can be attached to the assertion that all who are saved *are baptized by Christ to God?* On what principle of interpretation is it justifiable to reject the natural, common meaning of a word, when, at the same time, it perfectly accords with the

---

[173]*Contra Hares.* L. ii. C. xxii

scope of the passage, and to adopt a figurative meaning which renders the passage unintelligible?

Secondly: This interpretation will not accord with the strain of the writer's discourse; or, in the words of Le Clerc, "We see nothing here concerning baptism; nor is there any thing relating to it in the immediately preceding or following words."[174]

Now this testimony, uncertain as it must be considered, at the best, and given at the close of the second century, is the first testimony that is insisted on by learned Paedobaptists.[175]Dr. Wall admits, "This is the first express mention we have met with of infants baptized."[176]But though Dr. Wall calls it *express mention,* it is generally given up as very uncertain.[177]

MONTHLY REVIEW. "The authorities produced are Justin Martyr and Irenaeus, in the second century. With respect to the testimony of Justin, it requires very considerable ingenuity to make it, in

---

[174]*Hist. Eccles.* Secul. ii. Ann. 180. & 33. p. 778.

[175]Passages have been sometimes cited from the Ecclesiastic Hierarchy, the Clementina, the Apostolic Constitutions, and the Questions and Responses to the Orthodox; but these works are denounced by the learned as decidedly spurious. See Drs. Cave, Wall, Mosheim and Maclaine.

[176]*Hist. of Inf. Bap.* Part i. C. iii. p. 16.

[177]See particularly, VENEMAE *Hist. Eccles.* Tom. iii. Secul. ii. & 109.

any view, an argument in favor of infant baptism. There is a passage in Irenaeus more to the purpose; *but the passage is equivocal.*"[178]

The first Christian writer in the beginning of the third century, Tertullian of Carthage, the oldest Latin father whose writings are extant, opposed the baptism of infants, which in the words of Professor Venema, "He certainly would not have done, if it had been a tradition, and a public custom of the church, seeing he was very tenacious of traditions; nor had it been a tradition, would he have failed to mention it."[179] His words lead us to conclude that infant baptism was then a novel practice, just beginning and approved by very few.

In his treatise on baptism, against the Quintilianists, after condemning rash baptisms, and maintaining the propriety and advantages of delay, especially in the case of little children, he proceeds thus: "What necessity is there, that sponsors should be brought into danger; since, by reason of death, they may fail in their engagements, or be disappointed by the intervention of a bad disposition? Our Lord indeed says, 'Forbid them not to come to me.' But let them come when they are growing up - when they are learning - when they are taught for what purpose they come. Let them be made Christians when they are able to know Christ. Why does that innocent age hasten to baptism?"[180]

Several quotations concerning infant baptism have been made from the writings of Origen, who flourished in the former part of the third century. But his original works are not now extant. These quotations are taken from a very corrupt Latin version, made by

---

[178] For May, 1784, p. 394.

[179] *Hist. Eccles.* Secul. ii. & 108.

[180] *Lib. de Baptismo*, C. xviii.

Ruffinus, who, as Quenstedius observes, "has used so great a liberty (as he himself acknowledges in his prefaces, and for which Jerome reproves him) that he retrenched, added, and altered whatever he considered as deserving to be cashiered, added or changed; so that the reader is frequently uncertain whether he read Origen or Ruffinus."[181] And Grotius, also, concerning the sentiments of Origen, says, "Some things ascribed to him were penned by an uncertain author, and some things were interpolated. What Origen thought about the final punishment of the wicked is difficult from his writings to be asserted, all things are so interpolated by Ruffinus."[182]

The only passage from the Greek of Origen which is produced in proof of this practice, contains a clause which represents the infants as *desiring the sincere milk of the word.* Therefore Dr. Wall acknowledges that this does "very much puzzle the cause, and make it doubtful whether Origen be to be there understood of infants in age, or of such Christian men as are endued with the innocence and simplicity of infants."[183]

This practice, however, probably commenced in the latter part of the second century, and gradually gained ground in the third. As the sentiment prevailed that baptism was necessary to salvation, parents became more anxious to have their children baptized, especially when sick and in danger of death.

VITRINGA. "The ancient Christian church, from the highest antiquity, after the apostolic times, appears generally to have thought that baptism is absolutely necessary for all that would be saved by the grace of

---

[181]*Dialog, de Patriis Illust. Doct. Script. Virorum,* p. 632.

[182]Apud Poli *Synops.* ad Matt. 19:14 and 25:46.

[183]*Hist. of Inf. Bap.* Part i. p. 32.

Jesus Christ. It was, therefore, customary, in the ancient church, if infants were greatly afflicted, and in danger of death, and if parents were affected with a singular concern about the salvation of their children, to present their infants, or children, in their minority, to the bishop to be baptized. But if these reasons did not urge them, they thought it better, and more for the interest of minors, that their baptism should be deferred till they arrived at a more advanced age; which custom was not yet abolished in the time of Augustine, though he vehemently urged the necessity of baptism, while, with all his might, he defended the doctrines of grace against Pelagius."[184]

SALMASIUS. "An opinion prevailed that no one could be saved without being baptized; and *for that reason, the custom arose of baptizing infants.*"[185]

So unsettled, however, was the practice in Africa, in the middle of the third century, that, at the suggestion of Fidus, an African bishop, it was made a question before the council of Carthage, in which Cyprian presided, whether infants might be baptized before the eighth day. The council decided in the affirmative, for the following reasons:

"The mercy and grace of God should be denied to none. For if the Lord says in his gospel, 'The Son of man is not come to destroy men's lives, but to save them,' how ought we to do our utmost that no soul be lost. Spiritual circumcision should not be impeded by carnal circumcision. If even to the foulest offenders, when they afterwards believe, remission of sins is granted, and none is prohibited from baptism and grace, how much more should an infant be admitted. Besides God would be a respecter of persons if he denied to infants what he grants to

---

[184]*Observat. Sac.* Tom. i. L. ii. C. vi. & 9.

[185]*Epist. ad Justum Pacium.*

adults. Did not the prophet Elisha lie upon a child, and put his mouth on his mouth, and his eyes on his eyes, and his hands on his hands? Now the spiritual sense of this is that infants are equal to men. But if you refuse to baptize them, you destroy this equality and are partial."[186]

We here see the primitive grounds of infant baptism, and from this reasoning, may form some idea of the wisdom and judgment of that "holy assembly" - the most ancient bulwark of Paedobaptism - on whose integrity and infallibility Mr. Milner seems almost disposed to rest the whole defense of the cause.

Let us proceed to the fourth century. Even at this period, we find Gregory Nazianzen, bishop of Constantinople, "metropolitan of all Greece and the oracle of the catholic world," expressing himself, on the subject of infant baptism, in the following words: "But say some, what is your opinion of infants, who are not capable of judging either of the grace of baptism, or of the damage sustained by the want of it; shall we baptize them too? By all means, *if there be any apparent danger.* For it were better, that they were sanctified, without knowing it, than that they should die without being sealed and initiated. *As for others,* I give my opinion, that when they are three years of age or thereabouts (for then they are able to hear and answer some of the mystical words, and although they do not fully understand, they may receive impressions), they be sanctified, both soul and body, by the great mystery of initiation."[187]

It is evident, however, from the writings of Ambrose, Chrysostom, Jerome and Augustine, that, in the latter part of the fourth century and the beginning of the fifth, infant baptism very generally

---

[186]CYPRIAN, *Epist.* lxvi. ad Fidum.

[187]In Robinson's *Hist. of Bap.* C. xxiv.

prevailed, - so much so that Augustine, the latest of those writers, adduced it in proof of the doctrine of original sin, in these words: - "Infant baptism the whole church practices; it was not instituted by councils, but was ever in use;" and his opponent Pelagius admitted, that "baptism ought to be administered to infants" - knowing probably, that by stemming the popular torrent, he should lose more, in point of credit, than he should gain in point of argument.

When Augustine says that the whole church practiced infant baptism, did he mean that this was *the universal practice of the church?*

The testimonies which have been already produced, and the well known fact that through the whole of his life he found it necessary to urge and enforce the baptism of infants, renders this interpretation inadmissible. We must conclude that infant baptism, in the time of Augustine, though not yet considered a necessary duty, was generally tolerated, nor ever refused to those parents who desired it for their children. Further than this it is impossible to stretch the meaning of Augustine without making him contradict his contemporaries and himself.

That he should suppose this practice to have been "ever in use," is not strange, when we consider that, in the words of Hospinian, "in the time of Augustine, it was commonly believed that whatever was received by the church as a devotional custom, proceeded from apostolical tradition, and the doctrine of the Holy Spirit."[188]

But however prevalent infant baptism had become in the time of Augustine, he thought it would not be amiss to instigate the Milevitan council, to explain and encourage the practice a little, in the following gentle and persuasive terms: - "It is the pleasure of all the bishops present in this holy synod to order that whoever denieth that infants newly born

---

[188]*Hist. Sacram.* L. ii. p. 41.

A nineteenth century woodcut of Lal Bazaar Chapel

A twentieth century postcard sketch of Lal Bazaar Chapel
(By Rathin Mitra)

A nineteenth century sketch of the baptismal of Lal Bazaar Chapel
(By John Brown Myers)

A recent photo of the baptismal covering at Carey Baptist Church
(Formerly Lal Bazaar Chapel)

PASTORS OF CAREY BAPTIST CHURCH

REV. WILLIAM CAREY	. . . .	
JOSHUA MARSHMAN	. . . .	1805
WILLIAM WARD	. . . .	1805
JOHN C. MASON	. . . .	1812
EUSTACE CAREY	. . . .	1815-1813
WILLIAM ROBINSON	. . . .	1825
ALBERT BAYNE	. . . .	1833
REV. W. W. EVANS	. . . .	1840-1844
REV. JAMES THOMAS	. . . .	1844-1853
JOHN SALE	. . . .	1855-1861 1863-1866
REV. JOHN ROBINSON	. . . .	1868-1876
REV. C. JORDAN	. . . .	1872-1873
REV. C. C. BROWN	. . . .	1875-1876
REV. H. G. BLACKIE	. . . .	1877-1879
REV. G. H. HOOK	. . . .	1880-1924
REV. THORNTON HOWIE	. . . .	1924-1930 1936
REV. W. CRAIG EADIE	. . . .	1931-1943
REV. G. H. BROWN	. . . .	1943-1945
REV. WALTER A. CORLETT	. . . .	1946-1969
PASTOR. FRED HILL	. . . .	1970
REV. WILLIAM L. PECK	. . . .	1971
REV. WILBUR S. SORLEY	. . . .	1972-1974
REV. S. B. THOMAS	. . . .	1975-1980
REV. LLOYD D. RAINE	. . . .	1980-1991
REV. JOSHUA C. MOSES	. . . .	1992-

CHURCH EVANGELISTS

REV. DINABANDHU DASS	. . . .	1925-1950
REV. ARCHIBALD SHEAR	. . . .	1957-1960
REV. SUBODH K. SAHU	. . . .	1962-1964

*A recent photo of the roster of former pastors
of Carey Baptist Church
(Formerly Lal Bazaar Chapel)*

The present-day sign outside of Carey Baptist Church, Calcutta

*A twentieth century memorial tablet commemorating Judson's baptism
in Carey Baptist Church*

of their mother are to be baptized, or saith that baptism is administered for the remission of their own sins, but not on account of original sin derived from Adam and to be expiated by the laver of regeneration, be accursed."[189]

His motives were at least humane; for he says in another place that "not only persons who have come to the use of reason, but also little children, and infants newly born, if they die without baptism, go into everlasting fire."[190]

---

[189]In Robinson's *Hist. of Bap.* C. xxiii.

[190]In Davye on *Baptism*, p. 67. "From this period, every century has presented a succession of witnesses to the truth of the Baptist sentiments, as well as numberless decrees of popes, and kings, and councils, denouncing the severest penalties on this 'pernicious sect.'"

Cardinal HOSIUS, *President of the Council of Trent.* "If the truth of religion were to be judged of by the readiness and cheerfulness which a man of any sect shows in suffering, then the opinion and persuasion of no sect can be truer or surer than that of the Anabaptists; since there have been none, for these twelve hundred years past, that have been more grievously punished, or that have more cheerfully and steadfastly undergone, and even offered themselves to, the most cruel sorts of punishment, than these people."

"The Anabaptists are a pernicious sect, of which kind the Waldensian brethren seem also to have been. Nor is this heresy a modern thing; for it existed in the time of Augustine." In Rees' *Reply to Walker,* p. 220' and apud Schyn *Hist. Mennonite.* p. 135.

Dr. MOSHEIM. "The true origin of that sect,

The correctness of these statements concerning the practice of the primitive church, is confirmed by the following testimonies; the first, furnished by an apostle, and the rest, as usual by Paedobaptist authors.

ST. PAUL. "As many of you as have been baptized into Christ, have put on Christ."[191]

ERASMUS. "Paul does not seem (in Rom. 5:14.) to treat about infants. - *It was not yet the custom for infants to be baptized.*"[192]

LUTHER. "It cannot be proved by the sacred scripture, that infant baptism was instituted by Christ, or begun by the first Christians after the apostles."[193]

---

which acquired the denomination of Anabaptists, by their administering anew the rite of baptism to those who came over to their communion, and derived that of *Mennonites* from the famous man, to whom they owe the greatest part of their present felicity, *is hid in the remotest depths of antiquity,* and is, of consequence, extremely difficult to be ascertained." *Eccles. Hist.* Vol iv. p. 439.

See also DANVERS on *Baptism,* REES' *Reply to Walker,* and Robinson's *History and Researches.*

Concerning Dr. Gill's supposed concession, that he was not able to find any instance of an opposer of infant baptism, from the fourth to the eleventh century, See Dr. BALDWIN'S *Series of Letters to Dr. Worcester,* Let. xxiv. p. 232.

[191] Gal. 3:27.

[192] *Annotat.* ad Rom. 5:14.

[193] In A. R.'s *Vanity of Infant Baptism,* Part ii. p. 8.

M. DE LA ROQUE. "The primitive church did not baptize infants: and the learned Grotius proves it, in his annotations on the Gospel."[194]

LUDOVICUS VIVES. "No one, in former times, was admitted to the sacred baptistery, except he was of age, understood what the mystical water meant, desired to be washed in it, and expressed that desire more than once."[195]

CHAMBERS. "It appears, that in the primitive times none were baptized but adults."[196]

Bp. BARLOW. "I do believe and know that there is neither precept nor example in scripture for paedobaptism, nor any just evidence for it, for about two hundred years after Christ."[197]

SALMASIUS and SUICERUS. "In the first two centuries, no one was baptized, except, being instructed in the faith and acquainted with the doctrine of Christ, he was able to profess himself a believer; because of those words, *He that believeth, and is baptized.*"[198]

M. FORMEY. "They baptized, from this time (the latter end of the second century), infants, as well as adults."[199]

---

[194]In Stennett's *Answer to Russen*, p. 188.

[195]*Annotat. in Aug. de Civ. Dei.* L. i. C. xxxvii.

[196]*Cyclopedia*, Art. *Baptism*.

[197]*Letter to Mr. J. Tombs.*

[198]*Epist. ad Justum Pacium. Thesaur. Eccles.* sub. voce. (*zunaxis*) Tom. ii. p. 1136.

[199]*Abridg. Eccles. Hist.* Vol. i. p. 33.

CURCELLOEUS. "*The baptism of infants, in the first two centuries after Christ, was altogether unknown;* but in the third and fourth, was allowed by some few. In the fifth and following ages, it was generally received. The custom of baptizing infants did not begin before the third age after Christ was born. *In the former ages, no trace of it appears,* - and it was introduced without the command of Christ."[200]

RIGALTIUS. "In the Acts of the Apostles, we read that both men and women were baptized, when they believed the gospel preached by Philip; without any mention being made of infants. *From the apostolic age, therefore, to the time of Tertullian, the matter is doubtful.*"[201]

VENEMA. "Tertullian has nowhere mentioned paedobaptism among the traditions of the church, nor even among the customs of the church, that were publicly received, and usually observed; nay, he plainly intimates that, in his time, it was yet a doubtful affair. Nothing can be affirmed with certainty, concerning the custom of the church before Tertullian; seeing there is not anywhere, in more ancient writers, that I know of, undoubted mention of infant baptism. Justin Martyr, in his second apology, when describing baptism, mentions only that of adults. I conclude, therefore, that paedobaptism cannot be certainly proved to have been practiced before the times of Tertullian; and that there were persons in his age who desired their infants might be baptized, especially when they were afraid of their dying without baptism; which opinion Tertullian opposed, and by so doing, he intimates that paedobaptism began to prevail. These are the things that may be affirmed, with apparent

---

[200]*Institut. Relig. Christ.* L. i. C. xii. *Dissert. Secund. de Pece, Orig.* & 56.

[201]In Stennett's *Answer to Russen,* p. 74.

certainty, concerning the antiquity of infant baptism, after the times of the apostles; *for more are maintained without solid foundation.*"[202]

GROTIUS. "It seems to me that the baptism of infants was, of old, much more frequently practiced in Africa than in Asia, or other parts of the world; and with a certain opinion of the greater necessity of it. For you will not find, in any of the councils, a more ancient mention of this custom than in the council of Carthage."[203]

EPISCOPIUS. "Paedobaptism was not accounted a necessary rite till it was determined so to be in the Milevitan council, held in the year four hundred and eighteen."[204]

Dr. DODDRIDGE. "It is indeed surprising that nothing more express is to be met with in antiquity upon this subject."[205]

But how was it possible that infant baptism could have been quietly introduced in the early ages of Christianity, unsupported by apostolic authority, and the previous practice of the church? To the declamations of Towgood and others on this subject, the Baptists think it quite sufficient to reply, by asking, how were episcopacy and infant communion, and the use of sponsors or god-parents,[206] and a great variety

---

[202] *Hist. Eccles.* Tom. iii. Secul. ii. & 108, 109.

[203] *Annotat.* in Matt. 19:14.

[204] *Institut. Theolog.* L. iv. C. xiv.

[205] *Lectures*, p. 522.

[206] Dr. WALL. "There is no time or age of the church, in which there is any appearance that infants were ordinarily baptized, without sponsors or god-fathers." *Def. of Hist.* & 22.

of usages and ceremonies, introduced, without "a whisper of opposition," and suffered to pave the way to the complete enthronement of the man of sin? The truth is, that as soon as the spirit of inspiration withdrew from the earth, a multitude of errors and corruptions rushed in and deluged the church. This is indeed mortifying to human nature, and apparently unaccountable; but the facts are never disputed, unless a favorite hypothesis is in danger. Consider the case of episcopacy. It can claim much higher authority than even infant baptism. For while the latter is not mentioned by any writer in the first two centuries, frequent references to episcopacy, or the three orders of bishops, priests, and deacons, occur in the writings of the second century, and even in the epistles of Ignatius, one of the apostolical fathers. Professor Campbell, *an opposer of episcopacy*, though he questions the integrity of the epistles of Ignatius, admits, that "before the middle of the second century, a subordination in the ecclesiastical polity, which may be called primitive episcopacy, and may be considered the first step of the hierarchy, began to prevail very generally throughout the Christian world."[207]

Suppose, therefore, that even the quotation from Irenaeus, at the close of the second century, and those from Origen, in the third, are admitted to be relevant and genuine (and these are the very earliest that are insisted on), what ground is gained by an anti-episcopalian Paedobaptist? But the case of infant communion deserves more particular consideration. The same evidence can be adduced, in favor of the antiquity of this practice, as of that of infant baptism. And in the article of opposition, infant communion has the decided advantage: For while there appears to have been some opposition to the introduction of infant baptism by Tertullian, Gregory Nazianzen, and others, nothing of the kind appears in the case of infant communion.

---

[207]*Eccles. Hist.* Sect. vii.

As these points, if established, must, in the minds of those who reject infant communion, completely invalidate the argument from antiquity, in favor of infant baptism, and as these points must be established by testimony, independently of argumentation, permit me to introduce the following quotations.

SALMUASIUS and SUICERUS. "Because the Eucharist was given to adult catechumens when they were washed with holy baptism, without any space of time intervening, this also was done to infants, *after paedobaptism was introduced*."[208]

BUDDOEUS. "It is manifest, that in the ancient church, it was usual to give the Eucharist to infants; which custom arose about the third century, and continued in the western church to the beginning of the twelfth century, as Quenstedius shows. This custom seems to have prevailed, first in the African church, and to have been propagated thence to other churches of the west. Certainly, we no where find it more frequently mentioned than in the writings of Cyprian, of Augustine, and of Paulinus. The error seems to have arisen from a false opinion concerning the absolute necessity of the Eucharist; and it has been observed by learned men, that this arose from the words of Christ, John 6:53, not well understood."[209]

HOSPINIANUS. "The Lord's supper was given to the infants of believers, in the time of Pope Innocent the first, of Cyprian, and of Augustine; as well in Europe, as in Asia and Africa, and that as necessary to salvation. Jerome, Augustine, and other fathers testify that they who

---

[208]*Thesaur. Eccles.* sub. voce *sunaxis.*

[209]*Theolog. Dogmat.* L. v. C. i. & 19.

were baptized, not only adults, but also infants, without any delay, received the Lord's supper in both kinds."[210]

CHILLINGWORTH. "St. Augustine, I am sure, held the communicating of infants as much apostolic tradition as the baptizing of them. The Eucharist's necessity for infants was taught by the consent of the eminent fathers of some ages, without any opposition from any of their contemporaries; and was delivered by them, not as doctors, but as witnesses; not as their opinion, but as apostolic tradition."[211]

Dr. PRIESTLEY. "It is remarkable, that, in all Christian antiquity, we always find that communion in the Lord's supper immediately followed baptism. And no such thing occurs, as that of any person having a right to one of these ordinances, and not to the other."[212]

VENEMA. "In the ancient church, those two sacraments (baptism and the Lord's supper) in respect of the subjects, were never separated, the one from the other. In the thirteenth century, baptized infants ceased to be admitted to the Eucharist, because it began to be administered under one kind."[213]

Dr. WALL. "That the Roman church, about the year one thousand, *entertaining the doctrine of transubstantiation,* let fall the custom of giving the holy elements to infants; and the other western churches mostly following their example, did the like, upon the same account; but

---

[210]*Hist. Sacram.* L. ii. C. ii. p. 51.

[211]*Relig. of Protest.* Answer to Pref. & 10, and Chap. iii. & 44.

[212]*Address on giving the Lord's Supper to Children,* p. 10.

[213]*Hist. Eccles.* Secul. ii. & 100; Secul. xii. & 164.

that the Greeks, not having the same doctrine, continued, and do still continue, the custom of communicating infants."[214]

HALLET. "The late Rev. Mr. Pierce has demonstrably proved that it was the ancient practice to give the Eucharist to children, in an unanswerable essay on this subject. And as no one has, after many years, attempted to answer him, I may well here take it for granted, that infants, in the primitive church, were admitted to the communion of Christians."[215]

Let me conclude this part of the discourse by inquiring, Why do not the advocates of infant baptism become advocates of infant communion? Is the scripture silent concerning the latter ordinance? It is equally silent concerning the former. Are infants incapable of remembering Christ, of examining themselves, and of discerning the Lord's body, which are required of those who receive the supper? They are equally incapable of repenting and believing, which are required of those who receive baptism. Every argument which is brought to prove that the requirement to examine one's self and discern the Lord's body, does not exclude them from the other ordinance.

Every argument also, which is urged in support of the one ordinance, may be urged, with equal plausibility, in support of the other. Ought infants to be baptized, because, under a former dispensation, they were circumcised? So also, because under a former dispensation they partook of the Passover,[216] they ought now to be admitted to

---

[214]*Hist. of Inf. Bap.* p. 517

[215]In Dr. Austin's *Econ. of the Church*, C. xii. p. 243

[216]After the tabernacle, where alone the Passover could be eaten, was established at Jerusalem, young children on

communion. Ought they to be baptized because they are connected with their parents, in covenant with God? For the same reason, they ought, with their parents, to be admitted to communion. Ought they to be baptized because they are members of the visible church? For the same reason, they ought to be admitted to communion. Ought they to be baptized because Christ commanded little children to be brought to him, and declared, that of such is the kingdom of heaven? For the same reason, they ought to be admitted to communion. Ought they to be baptized, because they are not unclean, but holy? For the same reason, they ought to be admitted to communion. Does it lessen the privileges which the church anciently enjoyed, to withhold baptism from infants? And does it not equally lessen those privileges, to debar infants from communion? Is it harsh and injurious to exclude infants from baptism? And is it not equally harsh and injurious to exclude them from communion?

Accordingly, Dr. Williams, the opponent of Mr. Booth, inquires, "Are not the same reasons which are brought for infant baptism, in like manner, applicable to infant communion? And will not the objections against the latter admit of the same answer as those against the former?"[217]

---

account of the distance, were not *required* to partake of the Passover, till they had attained the age of twelve years. But it would be gross to infer, that previously to that age, they had no right to partake of it, and did not partake, whenever presented. That they partook of the first Passover is admitted by all parties. See Dr. Th. Scott, on Exod. 12:43-45.

[217]Notes on Mr. Morrice's *Social Relig.* p. 78.

The reasons stated in both parts of this discourse lead us to the conclusion that, *the immersion of a professing believer, into the name of the Father, and of the Son, and of the Holy Ghost, is the only Christian baptism.*

"He that believeth and is baptized, shall be saved; but he that believeth not, shall be damned."[218] To believe in Christ is necessary to salvation; and to be baptized is the instituted method of professing our belief. It is, therefore, not only an infinitely important question to all men, whether they believe in Christ; but it is also a very important question to all Christians, whether they have been baptized.

If you love Christ, you cannot consider this question unimportant. You will be desirous of discovering the will of him whom you love, and of testifying your love, by joyfully obeying. *"If ye love me,"* said Jesus, *"keep my commandments."*[219] *"Ye are my friends, if ye do whatsoever I command you."*[220]

If, when your mind adverts to this question, you fear the consequences of an examination, and dread those sacrifices which a discovery that you have been mistaken may enforce on your conscience; or if you feel the influence of long established sentiments, and imagine that the subject is too dark and intricate for your investigation; look to the Son of God, who hesitated not to make the greatest sacrifices, and to endure the most painful sufferings for you; and look up to the Father of lights to send the Holy Spirit according to the promise of his Son, to guide you into all truth.

---

[218] Mark 16:16.

[219] John 14:15.

[220] John 15:14.

Especially, my brethren, diligently use the means of discovering the truth. Put yourselves in the way of evidence. Indulge free examination. Though the sun shines with perfect clearness, you will never see that light which others enjoy if you confine yourselves in a cavern which the beams of the sun cannot penetrate. Be assured that there is sufficient evidence on this subject, if you seek to discover it. But if your love for truth is not sufficiently strong to make you willing to labor for the discovery of evidence, God will probably leave you to be contented with error.

In order, therefore, to stimulate your minds to candid and energetic research, prize truth above all other things, be impressed with the conviction that nothing can compensate you for the loss of truth. "She is more precious than rubies, and all the things thou canst desire are not to be compared unto her."[221] She will keep you in the right way, the way of duty, of usefulness, of happiness. She will lead you to heaven. Seek her, therefore, as silver, and search for her, as for hid treasures.

Finally, *If any man desire to do the will of God, "he shall know of the doctrine, whether it be of God."* [222]

---

[221]Prov. 3:15.

[222]John 7:17.

The following is Wayland's historical notation on the background of the letter.[223] "On the 19th of February, 1812, Mr. and Mrs. Judson and Mr. and Mrs. Newell embarked at Salem, in the brig Caravan, Captain Heard, bound for Calcutta. They had been some time waiting for a fair wind; and, on the 18th, the long-expected change in the weather took place, and the passengers were in haste summoned on board. The brig remained, however, at anchor during the night, and on the following morning set sail with a favorable breeze.

The embarkation was sudden, and but few of their friends were aware of the time of their departure. Every comfort which kindness could suggest had, however, been previously provided. The captain was an intelligent and amiable gentleman, and they commenced their voyage under the most auspicious circumstances. The passage was pleasant, and on the 17th of June they arrived in Calcutta. Messrs. Nott, Hall, and Rice, who sailed about the same time in the Harmony, from Philadelphia, did not arrive until the 8th of the following month.

A controversy has, unfortunately, been carried on, respecting the embarkation at Salem, to which it is necessary very briefly to advert.

When Dr. Judson returned to this country, after thirty-three years' absence, he was greatly surprised at the change which had taken place in public opinion on the subject of missions. When he left for India, devout

---

[223]An abridgement of this letter may also be found in Francis Wayland's *Memoir of the Life and Labours of the Rev. Adoniram Judson, D.D.* (London: James Nisbet & Co., 1853, 2 Vols.), 1:93-95.

men were beginning to be interested in it; a few others looked with admiration at the romantic self-sacrifice which it exhibited; but I think I do not err in asserting that it was by many good men considered a hopeless undertaking. From my own personal knowledge, I can testify that, as late as Mrs. Ann Judson's second embarkation, it was with some difficulty that passages were procured for missionaries to India. When Dr. Judson returned, he found the cause of missions to the heathen the favorite object of Christian benevolence. It had entirely silenced opposition, and multiplied without limit the number of its friends. He was filled with admiration at what he saw, and felt assured that his highest anticipations of the progress of the cause had been more than realized.

In speaking on this subject, he, on one or two occasions, contrasted the circumstances of the pioneers, when they left their native country, with those of their brethren who were at the present day following them. I am confident that, in these remarks, he had not the most remote idea of undervaluing the kindness of his friends in Salem. In all his letters, as well as those of Mrs. Judson, this subject is never alluded to but in terms of affectionate gratitude. A use was, however, made of these remarks, which gave pain to the family of the late Dr. Worcester, and some of his friends at Salem. This was as far as possible from his intention. The contrast struck him forcibly, and, in speaking of it, he alluded to circumstances which happened to occur to him. He did not suppose that they would give pain to any one; for, as they existed in his mind, there was nothing either wrong or unkind associated with them.

The only event on the passage which has become specially worthy of note is the fact that Mr. Judson availed himself of this period of leisure to investigate anew the scriptural authority of infant-baptism. He was prompted to this course by two considerations. In the first place, he looked forward to the time when he should be surrounded by converts from heathenism. How should he treat their children and servants? Was he authorized to baptize them? And if so, what would be their relation to the Christian church afterwards? Besides this, he was going in the first instance to Serampore, to reside for a time with the Baptist missionaries. He felt the necessity for re-examining the subject, as he expected to be called upon by them to defend his belief. In this latter respect, however, he found himself singularly disappointed; for the gentlemen at Serampore made it a matter of principle never to introduce the subject of their peculiar belief to any of their brethren of other denominations who happened to be their guests.

As it seems proper to allow Mr. Judson to explain the reasons for his change of sentiment, I shall here insert a large part of his letter to the Third Church in Plymouth...

DEARLY BELOVED IN OUR COMMON LORD,

When I remember my early connection with your beloved church, the pleasant seasons which I formerly enjoyed with many dear individuals, the interest which you took in my welfare, and the affection with which you commended me to God, on leaving my native land for these Eastern shores, together with the certainty, that I shall see your faces no more, I cannot suppress my feelings, or restrain my tears.

I have several times had it in my heart to address you a few lines, but feared, that it would be presuming in me, who am but a youth, to call on the attention of those, who, in a spiritual sense, are men of war from their youth.

I have particularly desired to say a few things in regard to the change of sentiment, which I have experienced, since leaving you, to state some of the exercises of my mind on that subject, and to solicit a continuance of your candor and affectionate regards. And I hope, that this desire will appear to your minds a sufficient apology for addressing you at this time.

You will readily believe me, when I say, that on leaving my country, I little imagined, that I should ever become a Baptist. I had not indeed candidly examined the subject of baptism; but I had strong prejudices against the sect, that is every where spoken against.

It was on board the vessel, in prospect of my future life among the heathen, that I was led to investigate this important subject. I was going forth to proclaim the glad news of salvation through Jesus Christ. I hoped that my ministrations would be blessed to the conversion of souls. In that case, I felt that I should have no hesitation concerning my duty to the converts, it being plainly commanded in scripture, that such are to be baptized, and received into church fellowship. But how, thought I, am I to treat the unconverted children and domestics of the converts? Are they to be considered members of the church of Christ, by virtue of the conversion of the head of their family, or not? If they are, ought I not to treat them as such? After they are baptized, can I consistently set them aside, as aliens from the commonwealth of Israel, until they are readmitted? If they are not to be considered members of the church, can I consistently administer to them the initiating ordinance of the church?

If I adopt the Abrahamic covenant, and consider the Christian church a continuation of the Abrahamic or Jewish system, I must adopt the former part of the alternative. I must consider the children and domestics of professors, as members of the church, and treat them accordingly. Abraham, according to the terms of the covenant which God made with him, circumcised not only his own sons, but all the males, that were born in his house, or bought with money. His male descendants, in the line of Isaac and Jacob, were entitled to the same ordinance, by virtue of natural descent; and, together with their domestics, composed the ancient church, and were entitled to all its privileges. This is put beyond a doubt, by the single fact, that, in the Abrahamic community, or the society of Israel, there was no separate party, calling themselves, by way of distinction, *the church,* and saying to others, who were equally circumcised with themselves, Stand by, touch not the Passover, we are holier than you. No. All the members of the community, or nation, were of course members of the church. They were entitled to church membership, by birth or purchase. Their church membership was recognized, or they were initiated into the church, by circumcision; and in subsequent life, they partook of the Passover, which was the standing sacrament of the church analogous to the Lord's supper, and enjoyed all the rights and privileges of the church,

---

[224]If any one should be inclined to doubt the right of circumcised children to the Passover, let him consider the following:

WITSIUS. "In those companies (that partook of the passover) men and women sat down together, old men and young, whole and sick, masters and servants, in fine, every Jew that could eat a morsel of flesh, not excluding even young children." (*Econ. Foed.* L. iv. C. ix. & 14.

Dr. SCOTT. "Every person in each household, including women and children, ate this first Passover, none being excepted, but uncircumcised males; and afterwards all, who were not ceremonially unclean, partook of it. The women and children were not indeed commanded to go up to the tabernacle, where it was celebrated; but when they did, they joined in this sacred feast." Note on Exodus 12:43-45.

After the tabernacle, where alone the Passover could be eaten, was established at Jerusalem, young children, on account of distance, not on account of any personal disqualification were seldom brought to partake of the Passover. This neglect, however, was not allowed after they had attained the age of twelve years.

unless they were excommunicated, or, in scriptural language, cut off from the people.[224]

Now let me be consistent. Since I am exhorted to walk in the steps of father Abraham, let me follow him with the same faithfulness which procured him eminent praise. Let me not adopt some parts of his covenant, and reject others, as suits my own convenience, or accords with the notions, in which I have been educated. Nor let me complain for want of example and prescription. Behold the established church of England. She proves herself, in many respects, a worthy daughter of the Abrahamic or Jewish church. She receives into her charitable bosom, all the descendants of professors; and all those who, though not of her seed, belong to the families of professors; and these collectively come, in process of time, to comprise the whole nation. This is truly Abrahamic. This is the very system, which the ancestors of the Jewish race, and their succeeding rulers and priests uniformly maintained. And if I claim an interest in the Abrahamic covenant, and consider the Christian church a continuation of the Jewish, why should I hesitate to prove myself a true child of Abraham, and a consistent Christian, by adopting this system, in all its parts, and introducing it among the heathen?

But I considered again - How does this system accord with the account of the church of Christ, given in the New Testament? It appeared to me, from the manner in which this church commenced and was continued, from the character of its members, and in fine, from its whole economy, so far as detailed in the New Testament, that it was a company, consisting of select individuals, men and women, who gave credible evidence of being disciples of Christ; and that it had no regard to natural descent, or accidental connection with the families of professors.

When I proceeded to consider certain passages, which are thought to favor the Paedobaptist system, I found nothing satisfactory.

The sanctification, which St. Paul ascribes to the children of a believer I Cor. 7:14) I found that he ascribed to the unbelieving parent also; and herefore, whatever be the meaning of the passage, it could have no respect o church membership, or a right to church ordinances.

The declaration of St. Peter, "The promise is unto you and to your hildren, and to all that are afar off, even as many as the Lord our God hall call" (Acts 2:39) appeared not to bear at all on the point in hand, ecause the apostle does not command his hearers to have their children aptized, or acknowledged members of the church, but to repent and be aptized themselves. There is indeed a promise made to their children, nd to all others that God shall call; but it does not follow, that they were o procure the baptism of their children, or of those that were afar off, ntil they gave evidence that God had called them.

When Christ said, concerning little children, that "of such is the ingdom of heaven" (Mat. 19:14). it appeared to me, that his comparison ad respect, not to the age or size of little children, but to the humility nd docility which distinguish them from adults. This seemed to be put eyond a doubt, by his own explanation, in a similar passage, in which he ays, "Except ye be converted, and become as little children, ye shall not nter into the kingdom of heaven" (Mat. 18:3).

The baptism of households, which is mentioned in three instances, could not consider, as affording any evidence one way or the other, ecause, in a household, there may be infants and unbelieving domestics, nd there may not. Besides, I discovered some circumstances in each of he cases, which led me to conclude, that the members of the households vere real believers. They are expressly said to be so in the case of the jailer Acts. 16:34) and the same is evidently implied, in the case of Stephanas, vhen it is said, that they addicted themselves to the ministry of the saints ICor. 1:16; 16:15).

In a word, I could not find a single intimation, in the New Testament, that the children and domestics of believers were members of

103

the church, or entitled to any church ordinance, in consequence of th
profession of the head of their family. Everything discountenanced thi
idea. When baptism was spoken of, it was always in connection wit
believing. None but believers were commanded to be baptized; and it di
not appear to my mind that any others were baptized.

Here, then, appeared a striking difference between the Abrahami
and the Christian systems. The one recognized the membership of childrer
domestics and remote descendants of professors, and tended directly t
the establishment of a national religion. The other appeared to be a selectiv
system, acknowledging none, as members of the church, but such as gav
credible evidence of believing in Christ.

This led me to suspect, that these two systems, so evidently differen
could not be one and the same. And now the light began to dawn. Th
more I read, and the more I meditated on the subject, the more clearly i
appeared to me, that all my errors and difficulties had originated, i
confounding these two systems. I began to see, that since the very natur
and constitution of the church of Christ excluded infants and unregenerat
domestics, repentance and faith being always represented as necessary t
constitute a disciple, we had no right to expect any directions for, or an
examples of, the initiation of such unqualified persons into the church
To search for such directions and examples in the New Testament woul
be, as if the citizen of a republic should go to search his national code, fo
laws concerning the royal family which, by the very nature and constitutio
of a republic, is excluded. Suppose, that such a citizen, disappointed i
his search, should have recourse to the constitution and laws of
neighboring monarchy, for the desired information. This, it appeared t
me, would aptly represent the proceeding of those who, unable to find i
the New Testament, satisfactory proof of the right of infants, o
unregenerate domestics, should have recourse to the Abrahamic and Jewisl
codes.

At length, I adopted the following sentiments, concerning the two churches, and the concern which we have, at present, with the old dispensation. The Abrahamic church was preparatory to, and typical of, the Christian. The constitution was radically different; but it was, nevertheless, wisely adapted to answer the ends which God had in view. Natural descent or purchase was sufficient to introduce a person into his church; but still it appears, that, in every age, there were some who were truly pious; who embraced the gospel promise made to Abraham, before the covenant of circumcision was instituted; who also looked beyond the literal meaning of the requirements and promises, contained in that covenant, to the glorious things typified thereby, and thus exercised true faith in the coming Messiah, and in a better country, that is, the heavenly.

When the Messiah appeared, this preparatory and typical system, having answered its end, was destined to cease; and the Lord Jesus set up his kingdom on earth, the gospel church, composed of such only as repent and believe, or rather give credible evidence of these gracious exercises. The bar of separation between the Jews and the rest of the world was removed; thenceforth, none were to plead, that they had Abraham for their father; none were to rest in the covenant of circumcision, assured that if they did, Christ would profit them nothing; but it was distinctly declared, that thenceforth, there was neither Jew nor Greek, bond nor free, male nor female, but all were one in Christ (Gal. 3:28).

But whereas the Abrahamic system was typical of the Christian, so the spiritual meaning of the requirements and promises still remains in force. Thus, by looking beyond the letter, and regarding the spiritual import, according to the example of the pious Jews, a great part of the Old Testament is still applicable to us, though the New Testament is emphatically the Christian's law book. The natural seed of Abraham typifies the spiritual seed. The land of Canaan typifies the heavenly land. External circumcision typifies the circumcision of the heart, a circumcision made without hands, that is, the putting off the body of the sins of the flesh, even the circumcision of Christ (Col. 2:11). Believers, therefore, may embrace the promise of Canaan, in its spiritual application, as made to themselves, the spiritual seed, who have received the spiritual circumcision. Hence, also, all the devotional parts of the Old Testament, particularly the Psalms of David, the modern believer can make his own, adopting the language, as the genuine expressions of his own devout feelings.

In the same way are to be explained all the New Testament allusions to the ancient dispensation. When, for instance, the apostle says, "If ye be Christ's, then are ye Abraham's seed, and heirs according to the promise" (Gal. 3:29), we are to understand, not Abraham's natural seed, surely, but his spiritual seed, those who by faith as assimilated to him, and thus become his children; not heirs of the land of Canaan, in the literal acceptation of the words, but heirs of the blessing of justification by faith, concerning which the apostle had been discoursing, and consequently, of the spiritual Canaan, the city of the living God, the heavenly Jerusalem.

I cannot describe to you, dear brethren, the light and satisfaction which I obtained, in taking this view of the matter, in considering the two churches distinct, and in classing my ideas of each in their proper place. I became possessed of a key, that unlocked many a difficulty, which had long perplexed me. And the more I read the Bible, the more clearly I saw that this was the true system therein revealed.

But while I obtained light and satisfaction on one side, I was plunged in difficulty and distress on the other. If, thought I, this system is the true one, if the Christian church is not a continuation of the Jewish, if the covenant of circumcision is not precisely the covenant in which Christians now stand, the whole foundation of Paedobaptism is gone; there is no remaining ground for the administration of any church ordinance, to the children and domestics of professors; and it follows inevitably, that I, who was christened in infancy, on the faith of my parents, have never yet received Christian baptism. Must I, then, forsake my parents, the church with which I stand connected, the society under whose patronage I have come out, the companions of my missionary undertaking? Must I forfeit the good opinion of all my friends in my native land, occasioning grief to some, and provoking others to anger, and be regarded henceforth, by all my former dear acquaintance, as a weak, despicable Baptist, who has not sense enough to comprehend the connection between the Abrahamic and the Christian systems? All this was mortifying; it was hard to flesh and blood. But I thought again - It is better to be guided by the opinion of Christ, who is the truth, than by the opinion of men, however good, whom I know to be in an error. The praise of Christ is better than the praise of men. Let me cleave to Christ at all events, and prefer his favor above my chief joy.

There was another thing which greatly contributed, just at this time, to drive me to an extremity. I knew that I had been sprinkled in infancy, and that this had been deemed baptism. But throughout the whole New Testament, I could find nothing, that looked like sprinkling, in connection with the ordinance of baptism. It appeared to me, that if a plain person should, without any previous information on the subject, read through the New Testament, he would never get the idea, that baptism consisted in sprinkling. He would find, that baptism in all cases particularly described was administered in rivers, and that the parties are represented as going down into the water, and coming up out of the water, which they would not have been so foolish as to do for the purpose of sprinkling.

In regard to the word itself, which is translated baptism, a very little search convinced me that its plain, appropriate meaning was immersion or dipping; and though I read extensively on the subject, I could not find that any learned Paedobaptist had ever been able to produce an instance, from any Greek writer, in which it meant sprinkling, or anything but immersion, except in some figurative application, which could not be fairly brought into question. The Rev. Professor Campbell, D. D. of Scotland, the most learned Greek scholar and biblical critic of modern times, has the candor to declare (though he was no Baptist, and therefore, not to be suspected of partiality to the Baptist system) that the word was never, so far as he knew, employed in the sense of sprinkling, in any use, sacred or classical (See Note on Matt. 3:11).

But as my limits will not permit me to enter further into detail, on this part of the subject, I must beg leave to refer you to my Sermon,[225] a copy of which will accompany this letter. Suffice it to say, that whereas a consideration of the nature of the church convinced me, that I had never received Christian baptism, so a consideration of the nature of baptism convinced me that I had never been baptized at all, nothing being baptism but immersion.

Reduced to this extremity, what, dear brethren, could I do? I saw, that, in a double sense, I was unbaptized, and I felt the command of Christ press on my conscience. Now if I quieted my conscience in regard to my own personal baptism, and concluded, that on account of my peculiar circumstances, it was best to consult my own convenience, rather than the command of Christ, still the question would return, with redoubled force - How am I to treat the children and domestics of converted heathen? This was the beginning of all my difficulties, and this,

---

[225] "My Sermon" refers to the body of this book, pp. 3-96.

on Paedobaptist principles, I could not resolve by the Bible, or by any books that I consulted.

In order that you may feel the trying situation, in which I was placed, I beg you to make the case your own, particularly in regard to this one point, the treatment of the families of believers. You may thus be brought to feel the gripe of this Gordian knot, as I have felt it. It is true, you have not the prospect of converted heathen and their families to trouble you; yet permit me to submit the case of your own families. In what light do you consider and treat them? Do you strictly comply with the terms of the Abrahamic covenant? Does your conduct perfectly accord with the Abrahamic system? Do you baptize (if baptism is in the place of circumcision) your male children, and those only, on the eight day after their birth? Do you baptize your male domestics, and if you had slaves, would you have them also baptized? Still further - Do your consider your baptized children and servants members of the church, as circumcised Jewish children and servants were members of the Jewish church? Do you acknowledge their right to the Lord's supper, as soon at least, as they are capable; and do you feel your own obligations to require their attendance, and to discipline and exclude them, if they do not attend? Circumcision was the initiating ordinance of the Abrahamic or Jewish church; baptism has been regarded, in every age, and by all parties, as the initiating ordinance of the Christian church. Baptized persons are, therefore, members of the church. And if so, is it not wrong and dangerous to treat them as if they were not? I need not inform you, that among yourselves, and among all the Congregational churches in New England, children and servants, who were baptized on account of the head of their family, are considered no more members of the church than before - No more members of the church than others, that have not been baptized. They are, in fact, considered and treated as out of the church altogether, and as having no right to any further church privilege, until they give evidence of possessing religion, and make a personal public profession. Do you not hesitate, my brethren, at pursuing a course so anti-Abrahamic, so unscriptural? How can you plead the promise made to Abraham, when you so flagrantly violate the covenant in which they are contained, and depart from the course divinely prescribed in his family, and in subsequent generations? But on the other hand, if you adopt and practice the Abrahamic system, you will inevitably confound the church and the world; you will receive into the church multitudes who are destitute of those qualifications, which are represented, in the New Testament, as requisite to constitute a member of the kingdom which Christ set up; you will ultimately establish a national religion; and this will be as contrary to the system laid down in the New Testament, as your present system is to the Abrahamic.

Brethren and Fathers, I have now given you a slight sketch of the difficulties, in which I became involved, while contemplating my missionary work, and which forced me at last to adopt the Baptist system as alone consistent and scriptural. If I have done wrong herein, I shall be very grateful to any one who will point out my error - who will inform me what course I could have taken to extricate myself out of my difficulties, without becoming a Baptist. And in order to facilitate the matter, I beg leave to state the several points, on which I must obtain good satisfaction, or remain as I am.

1. Does it appear from the New Testament, that the unconverted children and servants of believers are members of the church of Christ according to the terms of the Abrahamic covenant? If this could be proved, it would go far towards proving that the Christian church is a continuation of the Jewish; but if this cannot be proved, it appears to me, that no little incidental similarities are sufficient to establish the point.

2. If the children and servants of believers are members of the church, by virtue of belonging to the families of professors, ought they

not, after being initiated into the church by baptism, to be considered and treated as members? Ought they not to be considered members of the Christian church, in the same manner, as the circumcised children and servants of the Jews were members of the Jewish church, and similarly entitled to the privileges and discipline of the church? And is it right or consistent to class them with aliens, until they come forward and join the church, to which it would seem, by the supposition, they had always belonged?

3. If the children and servants of believers are not real members of the church, by what right is one of the ordinances of the church, yea, even the initiating ordinance, administered to them? Do we discover any intimation, in the Old Testament, or the New, of any persons, who, not belonging to any church whatever, were yet entitled to the privileges of a church, and particularly to the ordinance of initiation, they being no more members of the church after they were initiated into it and acknowledged members, than others who were never thus initiated? And if a person should venture to maintain such a position, on any other subject than that of Paedobaptism, would not the soundness of his intellect be justly suspected?

4. If the children and servants of believers are not entitled to the ordinance of baptism, must not those who have been baptized, on the faith of their parents, or masters, necessarily regard their baptism as a nullity, and consider themselves, of course, in an unbaptized state? And when such persons believe in Christ, and hope that they have received divine grace, how can they refrain from obeying the express command of their Lord and Master?

Submitting these questions, dear Brethren, to your candid and impartial consideration, I take my leave. You will not, I hope, be displeased with any expressions in my letter, that may seem to bear hard on the system which you profess. Perhaps there are some such expressions. I have found it impossible to avoid them all, in stating my difficulties in their full force. And the same reasons which induced me to take up my pen at first, made me unwilling to soften and smooth those difficulties, through fear of giving offense. I have been sensible, that my change of sentiment would give much pain to many whom I loved and respected, to the members of the church I am now addressing, and to my honored father, your pastor. This reflection was the greatest trial attending my baptism. It was natural for me, therefore, to be desirous of showing you clearly the extremity to which I was reduced, and the potency of those arguments which constrained me to become a Baptist; hoping that you would, by that means, be led to sympathize with me in the exercises of mind that I have experienced, and be willing to admit that my conduct has not been the result of momentary caprice, or the still more reprehensible effect of interested and sinister motives. I solemnly profess to have done this thing from a single regard to truth and duty. I have not altered my sentiments on any point of doctrine, or Christian experience. My heart tells me, dear brethren, that I am still one with you, though we differ on the subject of baptism. May every blessing, temporal and spiritual, rest on you and on your children.

May the God of truth lead you and me into all the truth; and may the grace of our Lord Jesus Christ be with you all, is the prayer of your affectionate brother,

Adoniram Judson, Jun.
Rangoon, August 20, 1817."

There is satisfactory evidence, that believers' baptism constituted a part of primitive Christianity in the British isles. But in subsequent ages, it became extinct, being superseded by the baptism of infants. Immersion, however, maintained its ground until the middle of the seventeenth century, when the Westminster Assembly of Divines voted, by a majority of one, that immersion and sprinkling were indifferent. Previously to that period, the Baptists had formed churches in different parts of the country; and having always seen infants, when baptized, taken in the hands of the administrator, and laid under water, in the baptismal font, and not having much, if any, communication with the Baptists on the continent, they thought, of course, that a candidate for baptism, though a grown person, should be treated in the same manner, and laid backwards under the water. They were probably confirmed in this idea, by the phrase, "buried in baptism." The consequence has been, that all the Baptists in the world, who have sprung from the English Baptists, have practiced the backward posture.

But from the beginning, it was not so. In the apostolic times, the administrator placed his right hand on the head of the candidate, who then, under the pressure of the administrator's hand, bowed forward, aided by that genuflection, which instinctively comes to one's aid, when attempting to bow in that position, until his head was submerged, and then rose by his own effort. This appears from the figures sculptured in bronze and mosaic work, on the walls of the ancient baptisteries of Italy and Constantinople. Those figures represent John the Baptist leaning towards the river; his right hand on the head of the Saviour, as if pressing him down into the water; while the Saviour is about to bow down under the pressure of the hand of John.

The same is evident from the practice of the Greeks, the Armenians, and all the Oriental churches, who have not, like the

Christians of countries once overspread with the Roman Catholic heresy, exchanged immersion for sprinkling. All those Oriental churches practice immersion to the present day, and regard no other application of water as valid baptism. And in the case of adults, they uniformly baptize by bowing forward under the water. Such cases not unfrequently occur, though Paedobaptism has been long prevalent; for among the Jewish and Mahometan population of those countries, there are occasional converts to the Christian faith. The primitive mode of baptizing was preserved among the Waldenses and Albigenses also, as appears from the present practice of the German Baptists in the state of Pennsylvania and other parts of the United States. The eastern churches have, it is true, introduced trine immersion, and kneeling, and pouring on water, before or after immersion, and anointing with oil, and other adventitious ceremonies, by which the simplicity of the primitive mode has been marred, and its glory tarnished; but still their testimony in favor of immersion and the forward posture remains unimpaired.

The forward posture, as represented on the walls of ancient baptisteries, and practiced by the greater part of Christendom to the present day, is further confirmed by sundry notices in ancient authors now extant. One of the most pertinent is that of Tertullian, in the beginning of the third century, who says, "the Christians of his time were baptized by bowing down, with great simplicity, without pomp or many words."

It does not seem, that the ancient Christians, and those who have practiced the forward posture in subsequent ages, thought that they failed of reaching the full import of the phrase, "buried in baptism," though the common mode of burial is by placing the body in a supine posture: As in the quaint saying, that parables are not to be made to run upon all fours, so it is evident, that when a thing is completely covered up in the ground, it is buried, whatever the precise posture may be: It is evident, that if the forward posture in baptism obtained in the apostolic times, the apostle would have used the same figure and said, "buried in baptism."

It must not be intimated, that the present mode in Great Britain and the United States is, at all, rude or indecorous. It is too prevalent and too highly patronized to be regarded in that light. But when Orientals are first informed of our mode, they are filled with great surprise; and when they come to understand it, which they are slow to do, they cannot refrain from smiling, and, not unfrequently, involuntary laughter. When asked, however, whether it is not valid baptism, they will stop a moment, as if much amused with the oddity of the idea; but on second thought, will candidly admit - "Yes, it is certainly valid baptism, If they are put under water, they are certainly baptized; but it is so very, very curious."

It is the peculiar privilege of the Baptists, to have defended, in every age, the initiatory ordinance of the Christian church, and that, on the simple ground, that so far as the mode is concerned, immersion, however administered, and that alone is valid baptism. Other appendages may have occasionally been added; but they are not regarded as essential. Whether baptism is performed in a baptistery, in a river, or in the sea; whether the candidate be more or less clothed; whether he be immersed forward or backward, if he be immersed, he is baptized. There may be diversity of tastes and preferences; but the fundamental principle remains untouched. The mode generally practiced in this country is unquestionably valid and proper. It has also the great advantage of being sustained by prevailing usage. As, however, the evidence is decidedly in favor of the position, that the Lord Jesus was baptized by bowing forward under the hand of John; and as some individuals may prefer following, as nearly as possible, the footsteps of their Lord, I am sure, that all true Baptists will candidly and affectionately respond, We give others the same liberty which we claim for ourselves; let them be gratified.

Utica, June 7, 1846

POSTSCRIPT

Just as William Carey and the Serampore Mission were a great stimulus to many in the British Isles to support and even engage in overseas missionary outreach, so the labors of Adoniram Judson in Burma had a similar effect upon the United States. As this book reveals, however, Judson was not only a missionary practitioner, but also a scholar of no mean ability.

He had a firm grasp of the scriptural arguments in favor of believer's baptism as well as a clear understanding of the biblical problems involved in the defense of infant baptism. For instance, the Paedobaptist use of the Abrahamic covenant to defend their position involves a number of profound difficulties. All of the males of Abraham's household, free-born and slave, were to be circumcised. But, Judson astutely asks, does this mean that a converted slave-owner must baptize his unbelieving slaves? Moreover, the promise of possessing the land of Canaan was integral to God's covenant with Abraham. But no Christian, Judson rightly observes, dreams that being in Christ entails a plot of land in Palestine. Judson, it should be noted, wrote these words prior to the emergence of classical dispensationalism and its fallacious conviction that this aspect of the Abrahamic covenant would indeed be literally fulfilled.

Judson is also well acquainted with the history of this issue in the patristic era, and rightly notes that none of the earliest Church Fathers can be cited in defense of the Paedobaptist position. Then, he is aware of the profound theological difficulties involved in Paedobaptism. For example, infant baptism logically entails infant communion, but none of the evangelical advocates of the former defend the latter. But surely, Judson points out, there is a theological inconsistency here. Unless it is the case that infant baptism is not a biblical ordinance.

All in all, this is a soundly-argued, scripturally-based defense of believer's baptism. If it be considered in the spirit in which it was written, namely, a "candid and energetic research" to "prize truth above all things," it can still point men and women to the true nature of this much disputed ordinance: "the immersion of a professing believer, into the name of Father, and of the Son, and of the Holy Ghost, is the only Christian baptism."

There is one area, though, in which this defense is deficient. It admirably discusses the mode and subjects of baptism, but there is no significant treatment of the meaning of baptism. In fact, right at the beginning of the sermon Judson explicitly states that an examination of Christ's words in Matthew 28:19 suggests "two inquiries: What is baptism? and, To whom is baptism to be administered?" But, there is a third question to be asked: "What does baptism mean or signify?" Judson's omission of this question, though, is typical of his day, when Baptist reflections on the ordinance of baptism were largely limited to the questions of mode and subject. Early Baptists, however, were aware of this third question and its importance. For instance, those who drew up what is the first Calvinistic Baptist statement of faith, The First London Confession of Faith (1646), specified two major meanings behind believer's baptism. First, it depicts "that interest the saints have in the death, burial, and resurrection of Christ"; then, it affirms the hope in the resurrection of the body (Article 40). Inclusion of a discussion about baptism's meaning could in fact have strengthened Judson's argument. If, for instance, baptism bears witness to an individual's commitment to Christ, crucified, buried, and risen, it can be reasonably asked, how does a babe give such a witness?

What is especially noteworthy about Judson's treatise is its irenic spirit. The harsh tones that can be found in some Baptist literature on this subject are completely absent, and rightly so. It aims to convince through two of God's greatest gifts, scripture and reason. May all who read it, study it in the spirit in which Judson wrote it. And as God illumined Judson about this vital subject, may he also give illumination to all who read it with candour and an open mind.

Dr. Michael Haykin is currently Professor of Church History at Heritage Baptist College & Theological Seminary, Cambridge, Ontario, Canada. He is also the Editorial Director of Joshua Press, Dundas, Ontario, Canada

"When any person is known to be considering the new Religion, all his relations and acquaintances rise en masse; so that to get a new convert is like pulling out the eyetooth of a live tiger."

Adoniram Judson
American Missionary to Burma

Appendix 1
Letters written after the change on Baptism[226]

The extracts which follow from the letters of Mrs. Judson exhibit the manner in which she and Mr. Judson pursued their inquiries, and the loneliness into which their change of opinions by necessity plunged them:

From Mrs. Judson to a Friend.

September 7, 1812

"Can you, my dear Nancy, still love me, still desire to hear from me, when I tell you I have become a Baptist? If I judge from my own feelings, I answer, you will, and that my differing from you in those things which do not affect our salvation will not diminish your affection for me, or make you unconcerned for my welfare. You may, perhaps, think this change very sudden, as I have said nothing of it before; but, my dear girl, this alteration hath not been the work of an hour, a day, or a month. The subject has been maturely, candidly, and I hope prayerfully, examined for months.

An examination of the subject of baptism commenced on board the Caravan. As Mr. Judson was continuing the translation of the New Testament, which he began in America, he had many doubts respecting the meaning of the word *baptize*. This, with the idea of meeting the Baptists at Serampore, when he would wish to defend his own sentiments,

---

[226] These letters are taken directly from Francis Wayland's *Memoir of the Life and Labours of the Rev. Adoniram Judson, D.D.* (London: James Nisbet & Co., 1853, 2 Vols.) I:105-113

induced a more thorough examination of the foundation of the Paedobaptist system. The more he examined, the more his doubts increased; and, unwilling as he was to admit it, he was *afraid* the Baptists were right and he wrong. After we arrived at Calcutta, his attention was turned from this subject to the concerns of the mission, and the difficulties with government. But as his mind was still uneasy, he again renewed the subject. I felt afraid he would become a Baptist, and frequently urged the unhappy consequences if he should. But he said his duty compelled him to satisfy his own mind, and embrace those sentiments which appeared most concordant with Scripture. I always took the Paedobaptist side in reasoning with him, even after I was as doubtful of the truth of that system as he. We left Serampore to reside in Calcutta a week or two before the arrival of our brethren; and as we had nothing in particular to occupy our attention, we confined it exclusively to this subject. We procured the best authors on both sides, compared them with the Scriptures, examined and re-examined the sentiments of Baptists and Paedobaptists, and were finally compelled, from a conviction of truth, to embrace those of the former. Thus, my dear Nancy, we are confirmed Baptists, not because we wished to be, but because truth compelled us to be. We have endeavored to count the cost, and be prepared for the many severe trials resulting from this change of sentiment. We anticipate the loss of reputation, and of the affection and esteem of many of our American friends. But the most trying circumstances attending this change, and that which has caused most pain, is the separation which must take place between us and our dear missionary associates. Although we are attached to each other, and should doubtless live very happily together, yet the brethren do not think it best we should unite in one mission. These things, my dear Nancy, have caused us to weep and pour out our hearts in prayer to Him whose directions we so much wish and need. We feel that we are alone in the world, with no real friend but each other, no one on whom we can depend but God."

From Mrs. Judson to her Parents.

Isle of France, Port Louis, February 14, 1813.

"I will now, my dear parents and sisters, give you some account of our change of sentiment relative to the subject of baptism. Mr. Judson's doubts commenced on our passage from America. While translating the New Testament, in which he was engaged, he used frequently to say that the Baptists were right in their mode of administering the ordinance. Knowing that he should meet the Baptists at Serampore, he felt it important to attend to it more closely, to be able to defend his sentiments. After our arrival at Serampore, his mind for two or three weeks was so much taken up with missionary inquiries and our difficulties with government, as to prevent his attending to the subject of baptism. But as we were waiting the arrival of our brethren, and having nothing in particular to attend to, he again took up the subject. I tried to have him give it up, and rest satisfied in his old sentiments, and frequently told him, if he became a Baptist, *I would not.* He, however, said he felt it his duty to examine closely a subject on which he had so many doubts. After we removed to Calcutta, he found in the library in our chamber many books on both sides, which he determined to read candidly and prayerfully, and to hold fast, or embrace the truth, however mortifying, however great the sacrifice. I now commenced reading on the subject, with all my prejudices on the Paedobaptist side. We had with us Dr. Worcester's, Dr. Austin's, Peter Edwards's, and other Paedobaptist writings. But after closely examining the subject for several weeks, we were constrained to acknowledge that the truth appeared to lie on the

Baptists' side. It was extremely trying to reflect on the consequences of our becoming Baptists. We knew it would wound and grieve our dear Christian friends in America, that we should lose their approbation and esteem. We thought it probable the Commissioners would refuse to support us; and, what was more distressing than anything, we knew we must be separated from our missionary associates, and go alone to some heathen land. These things were very trying to us, and caused our hearts to bleed for anguish. We felt we had no home in this world, and no friend but each other. Our friends at Serampore were extremely surprised when we wrote them a letter requesting baptism as they had known nothing of our having had any doubts on the subject. We were baptized, on the 6th of September, in the Baptist chapel in Calcutta. Mr. J. preached a sermon at Calcutta on this subject soon after we were baptized, which, in compliance with the request of a number who heard it, he has been preparing for the press. Brother Rice was baptized several weeks after we were. It was a very great relief to our minds to have him join us, as we expected to be entirely alone in a mission."

The day after her baptism she wrote to her parents a further account of the progress of their inquiries on the subject, and mentions some additional particulars:

"Mr. Judson resolved to examine it candidly and prayerfully, let the result be what it would. No one in the mission family knew the state of his mind, as they never conversed with any of us on this subject. I was very fearful he would become a Baptist, and frequently suggested the unhappy consequences if he should. He always answered, that his duty compelled him to examine the subject and he hoped he should have a disposition to embrace the truth, though he paid dear for it. I always took the Paedobaptists' side in reasoning with him, although I was doubtful of the truth of their system as he. After we came to Calcutta, he devoted his whole time to reading on this subject, having obtained the best authors on both sides. After having examined and re-examined the subject, in every way possible, and comparing the sentiments of both Baptists and Paedobaptists with the Scriptures, he was compelled, from a conviction of the truth, to embrace those of the former. I confined my attention almost entirely to the Scriptures, comparing the Old with the New Testament, and tried to find something to favor infant-baptism, but was convinced it had no foundation there. I examined the covenant of circumcision, and could see no reason for concluding that baptism was to be administered to children because circumcision was. Thus, my dear parents and sisters, we are both confirmed Baptists, not because we wished to be, but because truth compelled us to be. A renunciation of our former sentiments has caused us more pain than anything which ever happened to us through our lives."

As soon as Mr. Judson had come to the conclusion indicated in the preceding letters, he of course informed the American Board of Commissioners for Foreign Missions of his change of sentiment on the subject of baptism. By the same conveyance he also communicated a knowledge of the facts to some of the Baptist clergymen in Boston and Salem. The following letters refer to this portion of our narrative:-

To the Rev. Dr. Baldwin, of Boston.

Calcutta, August 31, 1812.

"REV. AND DEAR SIR, I write you a line to express my grateful acknowledgments to you for the advantage I have derived from your publications on baptism particularly from your "Series of Letters;"

also to introduce the following copy of a letter which I forwarded last week to the Baptist missionaries at Serampore, and which you are at liberty to use as you think best,

I am, sir, with much affection and respect,

Your obliged friend and servant,

ADONIRAM JUDSON, JUN."

Calcutta, August 27, 1812.

TO THE REV. MESSRS. CAREY, MARSHMAN, AND WARD.

"As you have been ignorant of the late exercises of my mind on the subject of baptism the communication which I am about to make may occasion you some surprise. It is now about four months since I took the subject into serious and prayerful consideration. My inquiries, commenced during my passage from America, and after much laborious research and painful trial, which I shall not now detail, have issued in entire conviction, that *the immersion of a professing believer is the only Christian baptism.*

In these exercises I have not been alone. Mrs. Judson has been engaged in a similar examination, and has come to the same conclusion. Feeling therefore, that we are in an unbaptized state, we wish to profess our faith in Christ by being baptized in obedience to his sacred commands.

ADONIRAM JUDSON, JUN."

Calcutta, September 1, 1812.

"REV. SIR, After transmitting to the Rev. Dr. Worcester a copy of the above letter to the Baptist missionaries, I have, under date of this day, written him as follows:-

REV. AND DEAR SIR: My change of sentiments on the subject of baptism is considered by my missionary brethren as incompatible with my continuing their fellow-laborer in the mission which they contemplate on the Island of Madagascar; and it will, I presume, be considered by the Board of Commissioners as equally incompatible with my continuing their missionary. The Board will, undoubtedly, feel as unwilling to support a Baptist missionary as I feel to comply with their instructions, which particularly direct us to baptize '*credible believers with their households.*'

The dissolution of my connection with the Board of Commissioners, and a separation from my dear missionary brethren, I consider most distressing consequences of my late change of sentiments, and, indeed, the most distressing events which have ever befallen me. I have now the prospect before me of going alone to some distant island, unconnected with any society at present existing, from which I might be furnished with assistant laborers or pecuniary support. Whether the Baptist churches in America will compassionate my situation, I know not. I hope, therefore, that while my friends condemn what they deem a departure from the truth, they will at least pity me and pray for me.

With the same sentiments of affection and respect as ever,

I am, sir, your friend and servant,

ADONIRAM JUDSON, JUN."

Rev. Dr. Worcester, Corresponding Secretary of the American
Board of Commissioners for Foreign Missions.

"You will receive a letter from Dr. Marshman, accompanying this.
Should there be formed, in accordance with the ideas suggested therein,
a Baptist society for the support of a mission in these parts, *I shall be ready
to consider myself their missionary*; and remain, dear sir,

Your obliged friend and servant,
ADONIRAM JUDSON, JUN."

To the Rev. Dr. Bolles, Salem, Mass.

Calcutta, September 1, 1812.

"REV. SIR: I recollect that, during a short interview I had with
you in Salem, I suggested the formation of a society among the Baptists
in America for the support of foreign missions, in imitation of the
exertions of your English brethren. Little did I then expect to be
personally concerned in such an attempt.

Within a few months I have experienced an entire change of
sentiments on the subject of baptism. My doubts concerning the
correctness of my former system of belief commenced during my passage
from America to this country; and after many painful trials, which none
can know but those who are taught to relinquish a system in which they
had been educated, I settled down in the full persuasion that the
immersion of a professing believer in Christ is the only Christian
baptism.

Mrs. Judson is united with me in this persuasion. We have
signified our views and wishes to the Baptist missionaries at Serampore,
and expect to be baptized in this city next Lord's day.

A separation from my missionary brethren, and a dissolution of
my connection with the Board of Commissioners, seem to be necessary
consequences. The missionaries at Serampore are exerted to the utmost

of their ability in managing and supporting their extensive and complicated mission.

Under these circumstances I look to you. Alone, in this foreign heathen land, I make my appeal to those whom, with their permission, I will call *my Baptist brethren* in the United States.

With the advice of the brethren at Serampore, I am contemplating a mission on one of the eastern islands. They have lately sent their brother Chater to Ceylon, and their brother Robinson to Java. At present, Amboyna seems to present the most favorable opening. Fifty thousand souls are there perishing without the means of life; and the situation of the island is such that a mission there established might, with the blessing of God, be extended to the neighboring islands in those seas.

But should I go thither, it is a most painful reflection that I must go alone, and also uncertain of the means of support. But I will trust in God. He has frequently enabled me to praise his divine goodness, and will never forsake those who put their trust in him.

I am, dear sir,

Yours, in the Lord Jesus,

ADONIRAM JUDSON, JUN."

Extract of a Letter from Dr. Marshman, of Serampore, to Rev. Dr. Baldwin, of Boston, dated September 1, 1812.

"A note which brother Judson sent to brother Carey last Saturday has occasioned much reflection among us. In it he declares his belief that believers' baptism alone is the doctrine of the Scriptures, and requests to be baptized in the name of the Lord Jesus.

This unexpected circumstance seems to suggest many ideas. The change in the young man's mind respecting this ordinance of Christ, seems quite the effect of divine truth operating on the mind. It began when no Baptist was near (on board ship), and when he, in the conscientious discharge of his duty, was examining the subject in order to maintain what he then deemed truth on his arrival in Bengal. And so carefully did he conceal the workings of his mind from us, on his arrival, that he scarcely gave us a hint respecting them before he sent this note to brother Carey. This was not indeed very difficult for him to do, as we make it a point to guard against obtruding on missionary brethren of different sentiments any conversation relative to baptism.

This change, then, which I believe few who know brother Judson will impute to whim, or to anything besides sincere conviction, seems to point out something relative to the duty of our Baptist brethren with you, as it relates to the cause of missions. It can scarcely be expected that the Board of Commissioners will support a Baptist missionary, who cannot, of course, comply with their instructions, and baptize *whole households* on the parents' faith; and it is certain that the young man ought not to be left to perish for want, merely because he loved the truth more than father or mother; nor be compelled to give up missionary work for want of support therein. Now, though we should certainly interfere to prevent a circumstance like this happening, particularly as we have given our Paedobaptist brother Newell, gone to the Isle of France, an order to draw there upon us should he be in distress, yet to say nothing of the missionary concerns already lying on us, and constantly enlarging, it seems as though Providence itself were raising up this young man, that you might at least partake of the zeal of our Congregational missionary brethren around you. I would wish, then, that you should share in the glorious work, by supporting him. Let us do whatsoever things are *becoming,* and whatsoever things are *lovely,* and leave the reverse of those for others. After God has thus given you a missionary of your own nation, faith, and order, without the help or knowledge of men, let me entreat you, and Dr. Messer, and brethren Bolles and Moriarty, humbly to accept the gift.

To you I am sure I need add no more than to beg you to give my cordial love to all our brethren around you.

I may probably write you again soon, and in the meantime remain yours, in the Lord,

JOSHUA MARSHMAN."

"*The greatest struggle in my theology has not been, oddly enough, the five points of Calvinism and the Reformed faith. I find these clear and well-defined from Genesis to Revelation. Rather, the thorn in my theological flesh has been baptism...As I look back to those days as a sincere and searching seminary student I often wonder if I was searching for the truth as honestly as I thought I was...*"

Fred A. Malone
A String of Pearls Unstrung, p.9

John 15 - pg. 08-09

...n Baptism describes almost identically my theological journey into "the baptism of disciples alone." Having served joyfully in paedobaptist churches, as did Judson, I also was surprised by Scripture in 1977 as a Presbyterian (PCA) pastor. This rejection of infant baptism required my sorrowful departure from the Presbyterian ministry and into the Baptist ministry. Subsequently, I wrote a brief defense of my change, as did Judson, published as "A String of Pearls Unstrung." This has been published by Founder's Press of Cape Coral, Florida. Entering Baptist ranks as a Reformed pastor has been a much more difficult path but with a much clearer theological conscience concerning the sacraments, by no means a minor doctrine as some try to make it.

Along with increasing numbers of Baptists rediscovering Reformed soteriology in Baptist and Southern Baptist history, coupled with the frustration of encountering opposition to these truths in many Baptist churches, there has been an increasing number of Baptists entering the Presbyterian church membership and ministry. And they are free to do so. However, some have entered paedobaptist membership and ministry, and I quote, more from "convenience...less hassles in ministry... better opportunity and security as a pastor...great Reformed minds

---

[227] This is the personal testimony of Dr. Fred Malone, pastor of First Baptist Church — Clinton, Louisiana. For a fuller treatment of his pilgrimage into believer's baptism from a paedobaptist background, see his booklet, *A String of Pearls Unstrung: A Theological Journey into Believer's Baptism* (Cape Coral: Florida: Founders Press, 1998).

believe in infant baptism, who am I to say they are wrong," rather than from a personal Biblical conviction concerning infant baptism. While one may understand why frustrated Baptists may enter paedobaptist communions as happier members, such reasons are unworthy for those entering the ministry by ordination vows subscribing to the Westminster Confession out of Biblical conviction concerning infant baptism.

Because of this situation, I welcome Judson's *Christian Baptism* as an encouragement to Baptists (members, seminary students, and ministers) to remain Baptist and to adopt a "pioneer missionary spirit" in order to build and rebuild sound Reformed and Baptist churches for the next generation. The courageous decision of Judson to submit his conscience to Scripture at all costs sets the standard for Biblical integrity regarding the doctrine of Baptism.

Several theological issues led to my change of theology. First, the household children's participation in the Passover Feast unsettled my rejection of paedocommunion, a view shared by many paedobaptist theologians. Although the New Testament requires self-examination before the Lord's Supper, the Passover texts seemed to require the participation of household children in the Lord's Supper just as Old Testament circumcision had seemed to require infant baptism. In that struggle, I realized that my hermeneutics were inconsistent.

The Reformed faith, based upon the regulative principle of worship, looks to New Testament priority for the elements of Christian worship, including the sacraments of baptism and the Lord's Supper. For the subjects of the Lord's Supper, room is made both for ministers who hold to paedocommunion (through Old Testament "good and necessary inference") and to disciple's only communion (from New Testament precept). However, for the subjects of baptism, "good and necessary inference" from the Old Testament takes priority over the New Testament precept and example, requiring subscription to paedobaptism for all Presbyterian ministers. No room is made for New Testament priority and precept for the subjects of baptism (i.e. disciples alone) as is made for subjects of communion. This inconsistent application of the regulative principle to the subjects of the Lord's Supper caused me to question why the same diversity was not allowed for baptism. New Testament revelation over Old Testament inference for a New Testament sacrament is the principle both for disciple's communion and for disciple's baptism.

Second, the classic paedobaptist explanation of covenant theology was that the children of Christians are considered in the Covenant of Grace (including the New Covenant administration), and are therefore entitled to the sign of baptism because Abraham's children were included in his covenant of circumcision. Since Christians, they say, are the children of Abraham, then we have the right and responsibility to baptize our infants as Abraham circumcised his.

The problem with this classic covenant theology is that it ignores clear New Testament revelation concerning who are the New Covenant "seed" of Abraham and what is the New Covenant itself as defined by Scripture. The final physical "seed" of Abraham is Jesus Christ, the one to whom the promises were made (Gal. 3:16-19). Only His "seed" receive the sign. His exclusive seed are those who are of faith (Gal. 3:7,29). Only through faith in Christ does one become Christ's "seed," and therefore Abraham's fulfilled "seed." Even if baptism were the direct typological fulfillment of circumcision (instead of heart circumcision according to the New Testament; Rom. 2:29; Phil. 3:3; 2 Cor. 1:22), then only Christ's seed of faith are entitled to it. Biblical baptism is the baptism of disciples alone. The New Covenant itself, as John Owen and Jonathan Edwards agreed, is effectual for every member. Many ignore that Jer. 31:31-34 and 32:40 describe every New Covenant member with a heart that fears God, has the law inscribed upon it, possesses the forgiveness of sins, and actually knows God. The New Covenant is a covenant of "realized blessings" in every member purchased by the effectual mediator of every covenant member. For this reason, the New Testament requires the confession of repentance and faith as a prerequisite for the baptism of New Covenant members; i.e. the baptism of disciples alone. It is true, as both Baptist and paedobaptists warn, that we cannot know the heart of any confessor infallibly. However, it is also true that no one in the New Testament was considered to be "in" the New Covenant and therefore entitled to baptism unless there was evidence of a covenant heart revealed in their repentance and faith.

This is why Jesus made and baptized disciples alone (John 4:1). This is why the church at Antioch was literally called "the disciples," the first place they were called "Christians" (Acts 11:26). This is why the term "the disciples" was a common and significant designation of the church throughout the Book of Acts (1:15; 6:1-2; 9:1, 19, 25-26; 13:52; 14:20,22,28; 15:10; 18:23,27; 20:27). This designation means that the church was made of disciples alone; that is, those who had been baptized upon profession of faith.

Adoniram Judson's work on baptism is just as relevant today as it was when he wrote it. In a day when the Reformed faith is being rediscovered by Baptists, it is my hope and prayer that it will cause many of them to slow down before accepting infant baptism as an integral part of the Reformed faith. Rather, it is my hope that Judson will inspire many to endure hardship and to become "Baptist pioneers and missionaries" as we seek to build Biblical churches on the new frontier of the third millennium. Soli Deo Gloria! Sola Discipulus!

"It is worth noting, incidentally, that Zwingli himself went through a period of profound uncertainty over the whole issue. On one occasion, he confessed, 'Nothing grieves me more than that at present I have to baptise children, for I know it ought not to be done.'"

Phil Arthur
Grace Magazine, March 1999, p.11

Appendix 3
The Testimony of an Almost Judson[228]

The history of any human mind is incomplete unless it affords us some knowledge of inward struggles in regard to the acquisition of truth and the performance of duty. One of these crises occurred in the life of Mr. Alexander, while he was president of the college; and we must interrupt the regular narrative, to give some account of his difficulties respecting Baptism. His own record of this is so extensive that it might even form a separate publication. For our present purposes we must endeavor to afford an honest representation of the whole, in the way partly of abridgment and partly of extract.

"About this time," says he, probably indicating some part of the years 1797, 1798, or 1799, "I fell into doubt respecting the authority of infant baptism. The origin of these doubts was in too rigid notions as to the purity of the church, with a belief that receiving infants had a corrupting tendency. I communicated my doubts very freely to my friend Mr. Lyle, and to Mr. Speece, and found that they had both been troubled by the same. We talked much privately on the subject, and often conversed with others in hope of getting some new light. At length Mr. Lyle and I determined to give up the practice of baptizing infants, until we should receive more light. This determination we publicly

---

[228] The following is taken directly from *The Life of Archibald Alexander, D.D.* by J.W. Alexander, D.D. (Harrisonburg, VA: Sprinkle Publications, 1991 [1854]) pp.204-224

communicated to our people, and left them to take such measures as they deemed expedient; but they seemed willing to await the issue. We also communicated to the Presbytery the state of our minds, and left them to do what seemed good in the case; but as they believed that we were sincerely desirous of arriving at the truth, they took no steps, and I believe made no record.

Things remained in this posture for more than a year. During this time I read much on both sides, and carried on a lengthened correspondence, particularly with Dr. Hodge. Two considerations kept me back from joining the Baptists. The first was that the universal prevalence of infant baptism, as early as the fourth and fifth centuries, was unaccountable on the supposition that no such practice existed in the times of the apostles. The other was, that if the Baptists are right, they are the only Christian church on earth, and all other denominations are out of the visible church. Besides, I could not see how they could ever obtain a valid baptism."

Mr. Speece was however more precipitate, and having concluded that the Antipaedobaptists were right, strongly urged his friends to join him in going over. They endeavored to retard his progress, but his mind was naturally inclined to peremptory conclusions, and impatient of dubiety. One Sunday morning, therefore, he went to a Baptist meeting, held within two miles of the college, and without having given notice of his intention, was there re-baptized by immersion. On his return he seemed much satisfied with what he had done. The church soon licensed him to preach, and he began to go about the country with his Baptist brethren. "He attended an Association in Cumberland, where he preached; some of the ministers informed him that he aimed well, but that if he would do execution he 'must put to more powder.' They gloried much in their acquisition, and the day was often fixed by public rumor for my baptism and that of Mr. Lyle. It was evident, however, that Mr.

Speece was not perfectly happy in his new connection; yet he said nothing."

"I determined now," says he, "to begin anew the examination of the subject, and to follow the evidence which I might discover, to whatever point it might lead me. I had been too much disposed to reject certain kinds of evidence, as tending to favor the superstitions of popery, but now I resolved to give to every species of evidence and argument its due weight, and to abide by the consequences. Accordingly I applied my mind to the subject with great intensity. One night I slept none, but spent the whole time in pursuing a train of reasoning on this subject.

I began with the historical proofs of the early existence of this practice. At the beginning of the fifth century infant baptism was undoubtedly universal. This is evident from the frequent mention of the subject by many writers, while none can be found who doubted of its lawfulness. When Augustine urged on Pelagius that the denial of original sin would lead to the denial of infant baptism, Pelagius rejected with horror the thought of withholding baptism from children, and declared that he had never known or heard of any heretic who denied it. The practice had not been brought in recently, or the change would have been known to such men as Augustine, Jerome and Pelagius.

But we have other testimonies to the universality of the practice. About the middle of this century a council was held at Carthage, over which Cyprian the martyr presided. A question was here propounded by a presbyter named Fidus, respecting the proper time of administering this sacrament to infants. The doubt was, whether it should be deferred till the eighth day, as in the case of circumcision, or should be administered at an earlier time. The opinion of the council, consisting of more than sixty bishops, was unanimous, that it was unnecessary to wait, but that the ordinance might be administered at any time after birth. Now when an incidental question arises and is discussed, relative to the baptism of infants, and there is yet no intimation of any doubt being entertained respecting the lawfulness of the thing itself, it furnishes far stronger evidence that all received the practice without dissent, than if the same council had given a unanimous decision in favor of the practice; for this would have induced a suspicion that some must have denied or doubted the practice, in order to make it necessary that such an opinion should be formally expressed.

We must go a step further. Origen was born and grew up to manhood before the close of the second century, though he wrote and flourished in the former part of the third century. Origen was a man of extraordinary learning, and possessed a memory which retained almost every thing he ever acquired. In several places of his writings, he mentions infant baptism, but does not speak of it as a new thing, lately brought in, but declares that it had been handed down by tradition from the Apostles. But if it had sprung up after the Apostles' days, it must have been so near to Origen's time, that he could not be ignorant of the fact. A universal change in a public and interesting ordinance, could not have taken place in a very short time. Some churches, at least for a while, would have adhered to the Apostolic practice. Some discussion must have occurred. This would have drawn attention to the subject; and such a man as Origen, living as he did the greater part of his time in Palestine, could not have been ignorant of so great a change in the subjects of baptism, if it had been introduced after the death of John. Suppose that some one in our day should pretend that infant baptism was not practiced by the Reformers, Luther, Zwingle and Calvin. Though we are separated from them by an interval the double of that which intervened between John and Origen, yet would any learned man now be at a loss to know the truth of the facts in question? If infant baptism arose and became universal before the time of Origen, or rather the time to which his knowledge extended, it must have originated very near to the times of the Apostles, and its spread must have been exceedingly rapid, and at the same time marvelously silent; for in little more than half a century it was accomplished, and yet learned men, living at the close of that short period, knew nothing of the change, but ignorantly supposed that the practice had been actually derived from the Apostles.

That this is the genuine testimony of Origen [and not an addition of Rufinus] is confirmed by the state of the fact in the days of Cyprian, a little after his time. For the Council of Carthage, referred to above, must have believed that the practice came down from the Apostles; for they were of opinion that baptism came in the room of circumcision; as appears by the letter of Cyprian to Fidus. How so great a change could have taken place without any thing being said about it, or any opposition being offered, always appeared to me unaccountable. It seemed altogether reasonable to think, that if adult baptism had been the only baptism practiced by the Apostles, and by all churches in the age immediately subsequent to their time, in the many countries of the world over which Christianity had extended itself, it would be scarcely possible that in the short space of three or four hundred years, there should not be found a single church upon earth which adhered to the primitive practice. And as to the fact of the universal prevalence of infant baptism in Asia, Africa and Europe, as early as the time of Augustine, in the beginning of the fifth century, even the Baptists do not pretend to dispute.

But we must carry up the universal practice to a much earlier period. When the system of Pelagius was charged with leading to the denial of infant baptism, he utterly rejected the consequence, and declared, as has been said above, that he had never heard of any, even the most daring heretic, who called in question the propriety of infant baptism. Now if it had been denied by any part of the church within a hundred years of his time, he who traveled so widely in Europe, Africa and Asia, and was well acquainted with the condition of those regions, must have known it.

I repeat it, such a change in the subjects of an important sacrament, which was the badge of Christian profession and the door of entrance into the visible Church, could not have been made without much discussion. Opinions may and often do spread rapidly, without attracting much attention, or leading to much controversy. But this cannot be the case in regard to a great religious rite, performed in the presence of the church. Let us suppose, that some time after the decease of the last Apostle, some judaizing teacher, not contented that under the Christian dispensation there was no place for the infants of believers, should have determined to extend to them the ordinance of baptism. With converts from Judaism he might have found it easy to satisfy them, that as the Christian Church was derived from the Jewish, and was enlarged in its extent and privileges, it could not be that infants, who had been included in all the preceding covenants of God with his people, should enjoy no privilege whatever in the Christian Church; that therefore as baptism signified the same thing emblematically as circumcision, and stood precisely in the same place in the Christian Church as circumcision in the Jewish, infants ought, by clear analogy, to be admitted to baptism. Suppose, I say, the person who first introduced infant baptism, to have used this argument with the Jewish converts. It would not be surprising if he should bring some of them over to his opinion. Suppose the practice to have commenced at Jerusalem or Antioch. It is a problem worthy of consideration by Antipaedobaptists, how long it would have taken to extend the practice throughout all the churches in the whole world. Could it without a miracle have been accomplished in one century? And let it be remembered, that the more rapid the progress, the greater the exertion demanded. If the change went on gradually, without exertion, the progress must have been slow, and a change so universal could not have taken place in one or even in two centuries. But if those advocating for infant baptism were very zealous and made use of great efforts to introduce the practice, there must have been a great running to and fro, many discourses delivered, and many writings circulated. Surely a change wrought in this way would have left its impression upon the literature and history of the age. How then does it happen, that not a vestige of these arguments and endeavors, nor any notice of them should have come down -- I do not say to our times -- but even to the times of Origen, less than a hundred years after the practice commenced?

But even supposing it possible that all documents relating to this universal change should have been irrecoverably lost, so that not the least hint of any author remains concerning it, is it not a marvelous thing that among so great a multitude of churches, planted by the Apostles and entrusted to their disciples and immediate successors, not one should adhere to what they must have known was the uniform practice of the Apostles? If the innovation was begun at Jerusalem, and was received by the churches in Judea, can any one bring himself to believe, when some advocate of the new practice came to Antioch, where Ignatius was bishop, or to Smyrna, where Polycarp presided, or to Rome where Clement, the companion of Paul, had his residence, that such a novelty would receive no opposition from these Apostolic men? Would they not have been as staunch for confining baptism to believers, as the Baptist churches now would be, if any should seek to persuade them to baptize their children? And with much more reason; for they could say to the innovator, 'However plausibly you may argue in the way of analogy, we *know* that the uniform practice of all the Apostles was different, and that in all the churches planted by them and their coadjutors, there never was an infant baptized. We have conversed with the Apostles, were instructed by them, and have labored with them, and can testify to all the churches that what is now attempted to be introduced is an innovation, unsanctioned by

Apostolic precept or practice.' And as such opposition would undoubtedly have been made by those holy men, would it not have had influence to retard the progress of the error?

It will manifestly not satisfy the demands of the case to fix the introduction of infant baptism so near to the days of the Apostles. We must come lower down in the second century. Let us then place the commencement of the practice in the latter part of this century. And as this is absolutely necessary to the maintenance of the hypotheses, so it is convenient on another account. Tertullian, the only man of antiquity who has uttered a word unfavorable to the institution, lived about this time. Indeed, if the usage was not Apostolic, it must have been introduced in the later part of the second century. Earlier it could not be, for reasons which are incontrovertible; later it could not be, for we find it soon afterwards so firmly established and so universally practiced, that such men as Origen and Cyprian had no knowledge of its being an innovation, but believed that it had been derived from the Apostles.

When I first read Tertullian's testimony, this hypothesis appeared very plausible; for it has been pertinently asked, how can it be supposed that such a man as Tertullian would oppose infant baptism, if it had been universally practiced from the time of the Apostles? But if the practice was just beginning to prevail, nothing would be more likely than that this learned but austere man should set his face against it, and dissuade from the practice. Whatever may be doubtful, one thing is certain, namely, that it was customary at this time to bring young infants to baptism, and that for certain reasons which he assigns, Tertullian dissuaded from the practice. But when the whole passage is impartially considered, it makes very little in favor of the opinion that infant baptism was a new thing, an innovation just commencing. If this had been the fact, it would undoubtedly have suited his purpose to mention it. But Tertullian had evidently adopted the opinion afterwards current, that sins committed after baptism could not easily be pardoned. This led many, among whom was the Emperor Constantine, to defer their baptism until the near approach of death. Tertullian did not confine his dissuasions to infants, but extended them to young persons generally, and to widows; which shows that his objection did not arise from the circumstance of infancy, but from the consideration stated before. From all that is said by the early fathers concerning infant baptism, I drew the conclusion that it had been generally practiced without any dispute having ever arisen respecting it. And it is certain that it must have been common before the time of Origen and Tertullian; for it could not have become general between that time and the time of Augustine without having been known; since that is a period of history in which we have many writers and much more detailed information respecting the affairs and customs of the Christian church than in the preceding period between the Apostles and the beginning of the third century. And that this practice did prevail in that earlier period may be gathered from the testimonies of Justin Martyr and Irenaeus.

Here then it appeared that infant baptism could be traced up to a period bordering on the Apostolic age. How could this be accounted for on the principles of the Baptists? Could it have crept in and become universal within a few years after the Apostles? Here I was brought to a stand, and though I had laid it down as a principle from which I would not depart, to receive no doctrine or practice for which there appeared no foundation in the Holy Scriptures, I had come to a state of mind in which it appeared much more probable that it had its origin with the Apostles than that it had been privily brought in afterwards. I was prepared, therefore, *to examine the Scriptures without any bias against the doctrine.* I could not but believe that if the Apostles had sanctioned the practice, some vestiges of it would be discernible in the New Testament. For, taking my stand at the period when all acknowledge it to have become universal, I had to admit that so far as relates to historical probability there was much more likelihood that silently and without dispute it should have descended from the Apostles, than that it should have come in and gained a universal prevalence in opposition to the practice of the Apostles. All the facts are in accordance with the former supposition; all are unaccountable upon the latter.

I asked myself whether there was any thing in Scripture which had an analogy with infant baptism. The right of circumcision immediately occurred to my mind, as bearing at least some resemblance to it. I had been wont to consider the argument founded on the assumption that baptism succeeded in the place of circumcision as weak and inconclusive, for it seemed to involve a begging of the question. But I was willing to examine how far the analogy between the two institutions extended. And the more I considered the subject the stronger did this analogy in the main points appear. Circumcision, as well as baptism, was a religious rite instituted by God himself. Circumcision had an emblematical or mystical signification; it evidently represented the regeneration of the heart; and here the import of the two rites appeared to be not only similar but identical; for all admitted that baptism sets forth emblematically the washing away of sin. Then as to the subjects of the two ordinances, both, in the case of adults, required faith in the recipient. Paul asserts that Abraham received the sign of circumcision, a seal of the faith which he had yet being uncircumcised. If a stranger wished to join the Israelitish church, he was required to be circumcised, and in order to this he must profess his faith in Jehovah, the God of Israel, and avow a resolution to comply with all the precepts of the Mosaic law; just as the adult heathen, when he applied for baptism, was required to profess his faith in Jesus Christ, and to promise obedience to his commands. Circumcision was the regular entrance into the Israelitish community, as baptism into the Christian church. From a view of these points of resemblance, one inference was clear, namely, that all the ridicule cast upon infant baptism is misplaced, because the very same might be cast on circumcision, of which the infant could know as little as of baptism. Again, the Jews esteemed circumcision a great privilege, and Paul admits that it was every way profitable. Now if there is nothing come in its place, then are the privileges of the Christian less than those of the Jew; but Paul teaches that the Gospel dispensation is by far the more glorious.

About this time a friend lent me a volume of Dr. Hammond's Works, in which I found a treatise on Infant Baptism. This presented the subject in a new light. The author, making little use of the common arguments, undertakes to derive the doctrine from two sources, neither of which is in the Bible, but which both serve to illustrate what is there. The first of these is Jewish Proselyte Baptism, the second is the practice of the primitive church. Not having read this treatise for nearly half a century, I cannot pretend to state the author's reasonings; but I will give my own views of the arguments derived from these sources.

When a law is given to any people, a knowledge of certain common and notorious things is presumed by the legislator; for to enter into a minute description of every circumstance would be tedious and cumbersome. A law of this State of New Jersey inflicts a heavy pecuniary mulct on one who is engaged in 'gill-fishing,' but does not define what sort of fishing this is. If it should be necessary, in some other country, to interpret this law, it would be requisite to refer to such documents as would show what was commonly understood by the term; and without such explanations the law would be unintelligible. So in England, there are laws against poaching, but to a common reader in this country, where no such offence does or can take place, explanation is indispensable. Many canons of the church can be understood only by a reference to the history of the times. If a law should be found in the Jewish code, directing proselytes from the heathen to be circumcised before admission to the privileges of the Israelitish church, one unacquainted with the Mosaic institutions would be at a loss to know whether this included infants; but if he should turn to the seventeenth chapter of Genesis he would see at once that infants as well as adults were intended. Here then the question arises, whether any custom existed among the Jews in our Savior's time, which would enable them to determine to whom baptism was to be administered, under the command, 'Go, proselyte all nations, baptizing them.' If the command had been, 'Go, circumcise all nations,' the case would be clear; but had the Jews been acquainted with the rite of baptism? I am aware that Dr. Owen, Dr. Gill and Dr. Jennings, with others deny that any such practice existed among the Jews, previously to the time of our Lord. But after weighing the evidence exhibited by Lightfoot, Selden, Hammond, Wall, and other writers profoundly versed in Hebrew antiquities, I am fully convinced that the rite of baptism was not a novelty among the Jews, when John began his ministry. If the rite had never been known before, it would have been necessary to explain minutely what the nature of the ceremony was, and not merely to designate it by a single word. When certain priests and Levites were sent from the Sanhedrim to John, to inquire who he was, there was no question about the rite itself, which would naturally have been the object of inquiry if they had never heard of it before; whereas the only query was about his authority to administer it. 'If thou art not the Messiah, Elias, or that prophet, why baptizest thou?' The testimony against proselyte baptism is purely negative, and may all be summed up in a single sentence. The practice is never mentioned by Philo or Josephus, Jewish writers who lived nearest to the time of Christ, nor by any other writer until the Talmud was written, two centuries or more after the Christian era. To this it may be answered, that mere negative testimony is in any case of very little weight, unless it can be shown that the witnesses had occasion to mention the fact if it had existed. Again, when any practice is once fully established and familiar to all, there is seldom any mention of it by writers sacred or profane. When any discussion of it arises, then of course it is frequently referred to. After the Israelites were fully settled in Canaan, we hear nothing of circumcision for centuries, while all admit that it was universally practiced. From the creation till the time of Moses we have no distinct mention of the Sabbath, and yet we know that from the beginning God blessed the Sabbath day and hallowed it. There is nothing said in the New Testament about the admission of proselytes to the Jewish religion from the heathen; and although Josephus mentions many who were proselyted, he enters into no description of the ceremonies observed at the admission of such. The traditionary laws of the Jews, giving a minute account of all the rites and ceremonies of the temple-service, were committed to writing in the Talmud. Here we have the most full and particular testimony concerning the ceremonies observed in making proselytes. Maimonides, one of the most learned of the Jewish rabbins, has given us a minute account of proselyte baptism."[229]

In detailing the arguments which influenced his conclusion on this important point, Mr. Alexander proceeds to consider the traces of infant baptism in the New Testament. But it would be unjust to give the reasoning in abridgment or extract. On another part of the subject he proceeds as follows:

"As to the mode of baptism, I hold it to be a dispute about a very trivial matter. The mere mode of applying water, when used emblematically and sacramentally, cannot be an affair of very serious importance, unless, indeed, the very mode of application be emblematical.

---

[229] The extended citation of Jewish authorities and Christian fathers, which follows in the manuscript, cannot be brought within the just limits of this memoir.

Thus in the Lord's Supper, it is of no consequence whether the bread is of wheat or barley, leavened or unleavened, but it is of importance that the bread be broken, because that action of breaking the bread is emblematical of the breaking of Christ's body, and cannot with propriety be omitted, as it is by the Romanists, who place an unbroken wafer on the tongue of the communicant. If immersion in water is that in the sacrament which is significant, then this action or mode, and no other, should be used. The Baptists have therefore endeavored to prove that baptism was intended to signify and represent the burial and resurrection of Jesus Christ, as a primary object, and then our death unto sin, and the like. But this is not the idea set forth in the Scriptures. They never speak of baptism as being a commemorative ordinance, like the Lord's Supper. They never represent the thing signified as being the burial and resurrection of Christ. It does indeed signify our spiritual burial and resurrection; that is to say, it signifies the washing of the soul from the impurities of sin. Baptism is every where represented in connection with the remission of sins.

If now it could be demonstrated that John baptized by a total immersion of the body, and that the Apostles did likewise, we should be no more obliged to use this mode, than to use unleavened bread at the Lord's Supper; being sure, nevertheless, that no other kind of bread could have been eaten at the Passover. We are no more bound to follow this mode than the mode of reclining on couches at the Lord's table; the latter being as important a mode as the manner of applying water to the body; unless, as I said before, the thing intended to be signified or represented in baptism, is held forth by the very action or mode of immersion, which can never be proved. We are at liberty, therefore, to depart from what we know was an original mode, provided that mode was only incidental and unconnected with the essential meaning of the sacrament.

But we have conceded too much. So far is it from being true, that all baptisms mentioned in the New Testament were by a total immersion of the body, it cannot be proved that this was the mode in a single instance. Here follows an argument on this head, which would not fall within our plan."

By this process of diligent inquiry his mind was at length brought to peace upon a subject which had given him great distress for as much, it is believed, as two years. He quietly resumed the practice of the church, in which he was joined by his friend and relative Mr. Lyle. And after a short time Mr. Speece returned to the bosom of the church, of which he remained for many years an ornament.

It is not without entertainment that we read the account of these events in the "History of the Rise and Progress of the Baptists in Virginia," by the Rev. Robert B. Semple. He is speaking of the Middle District Association.

"The sessions were as usual, until October, 1800, when they met at Tarwallet Meeting-House, in Cumberland County. This is said to have been one of the most unpleasant, and, indeed, confused meetings, that the Association had ever witnessed. The consequences did not subside for several years, as we shall presently show. It was at this session that Mr. Conrad Speece (now a Presbyterian preacher), who had been baptized in the course of the year, by elder James Saunders, was introduced as a Baptist preacher, and was found, both in the pulpit and private conference, agreeable and clever. He was a man of considerable learning, having been educated for a Presbyterian preacher. By reading some treatise on believers baptism, as 'tis said, he became convinced of the impropriety of infant baptism. After some time devoted to the study of the subject, he offered himself as a candidate for baptism, and was accordingly baptized by Mr. Saunders. Soon after this Association, he professed to be again convinced of the validity of infant sprinkling, and wrote a letter to Mr. Saunders, to that effect. He rejoined the Presbyterians, and has since continued with them. Of his motives it is difficult to judge. By some it was said that he was disgusted with the turbulent proceedings of the Association at this session; by others, that Mr. Speece was much disappointed on finding that Baptist preachers received little or no compensation for their ministerial services. It is, perhaps, more probable, that he found the general tenor of the manners and customs of the Baptists quite different from his own and those of his former associates. Finding his temper soured at the loss of society to which his habits were assimilated, and not able at once to accommodate himself to that into which he had now fallen, he was the more easily persuaded of the truth of principles, which but a few months previously he had renounced as erroneous and false. It has sometimes been made a question in private companies, whether it would not have been more wise, on this occasion, to have separated baptism and church membership. *There were at this time several other eminent Presbyterian preachers, halting between two opinions.* It was thought they were perfectly persuaded of the impropriety of infant baptism, and therefore did not for many years baptize a single child, but were averse to joining the Baptists, or, however, from some cause, did not do it. Now, say some, had one or more of these been baptized, without requiring them to become members of the Baptist Church, he could have baptized the rest, and they might have formed a society to themselves, in which the ordinances would have been preserved pure, although their church government and general manners would have been different from the other Baptists. These suggestions were wholly speculative; one thing however is certain, that when Mr. Speece deserted the Baptists, the scruples of all the others were quickly removed, and they resumed the absurd practice of sprinkling children. Of Speece we must say, we wish that he had either never submitted to baptism, or that, being baptized, he had not again turned away." pp. 197, 198.

"*The Church of England Catechism has in it, as some of you may remember, this question, 'What is required of persons to be baptized?' and the answer I was taught to give, and did give, was, 'Repentance, whereby they forsake sin, and faith, whereby they steadfastly believe the promises of God made to them in that sacrament.' I looked that answer up in the Bible, and I found it to be strictly correct as far as repentance and faith are concerned, and of course, when I afterwards became a Christian, I also became a Baptist; and here I am, and it is due to the Church of England Catechism that I am a Baptist. Having been brought up among Congregationalists, I had never looked into the matter in my life. I had thought myself to have been baptized as an infant; and so, when I was confronted with the question, 'What is required of persons to be baptized?' and I found that repentance and faith were required, I said to myself, 'Then I have not been baptized; that infant sprinkling of mine was a mistake; and please God that I ever have repentance and faith, I will be properly baptized'...It led me, however, as I believe, to follow the Scriptural teaching that repentance and faith are required before there can be any true baptism.*"

Charles Spurgeon
C. H. Spurgeon: The Early Years, p.38

Appendix 4
C.H. Spurgeon on Baptism[230]

BAPTISM is, we doubt not, immersion. This is taught by all Greek usage of the terms chosen by the spirit of inspiration to designate this action. It is admitted by almost every learned Paedobaptist that until the time of Christ the word *baptize* had no other meaning. It required that "the element encompass its object." Nor does the use of this word by heathen or Christian Greeks, in the ages immediately succeeding apostolic times, encourage the idea of a changed import adopted by inspired penmen, which some vainly imagine. Any one maintaining this change of import in inspired writ, is bound to prove that, in one or more instances, the word is divinely used in another sense, the previous import (immersion) being certainly inadmissible. There is not such an occurrence. On Paedobaptist testimony, the immersion of "pots, cups, brasen vessels," yea, of beds, was a Jewish custom, in order to cleanliness, or purification from ceremonial defilement. So also immersion on returning from the market, or from a crowd, and often by many before eating. Facts, on Paedobaptist testimony, prove that the rich Pharisee, who expected our Saviour to baptize himself before eating, might have ample provision for immersion, and that the climate, clothing, and habits of Syrian Jews, made them ever ready for the practice of immersion without indelicacy or injury. Consequently the record of great numbers baptized by John, or by the disciples of Jesus, and the non-record as to

---

[230] The following article was added by C.H.Spurgeon as an appendix to his republished edition of *A Body of Divinity* by Thomas Watson, a Puritan paedobaptist. It was republished in London in 1890 by Passmore & Alabaster.

whether or how they changed their garments, proves nothing against immersion. Bathings in the Jordan, now annually and more frequently taking place, testify its present suitability for immersion; nor can the idea that a river, flowing hundreds of miles, was either too deep or too shallow for immersion, be rationally entertained. The sufficiency of water and baths in Jerusalem, Samaria, and Damascus, for the immersion of those whose baptism in the oracles of God is recorded, has abundant Paedobaptist and every other acknowledgment. The baptism of Israel in the cloud and in the sea, and the baptism of the Spirit by Christ, are not literal baptisms in water. By the sea and the cloud unitedly the children of Israel were covered. That the disciples as to their bodies, on the day of Pentecost, were not encompassed with the emblematic fire, is incapable of proof, whilst all admit that their souls were, as it were, immersed in the divine Spirit. The fulfilment of a predicted and abundant pouring might therefore constitute an immersion as to body and soul, or that which by no other word can be more properly designated. A prediction of the sprinkling of water, or pouring out of the Spirit by the divine Being on men, is no proof that the word which, in the New Testament, describes the divinely enjoined action of man towards man, is either sprinkling, or pouring, or immersion. The expression of Peter, "Can any man forbid water?" cannot be proved to mean more than, "Can any man forbid baptism?" nor dare any who are regardful of truth affirm that the jail at Philippi was not, like other Eastern jails, supplied with a bath.

  The fact that the Greek words *baptize, baptisma,* and *baptismos,* underwent no change of import when used by the inspired writers, is evident from such expressions as, that John baptized "in Jordan," and "in Aenon, near to Salim, *because there was much water there;*" that Philip and the eunuch "went down both into the water;" that we are *buried* with Christ "by baptism," and "in baptism," in which also we "are risen with him." If the words buried and risen are here used figuratively, there is an allusion to the literal immersion and emersion which had taken place. The calling of the overwhelming sufferings of Christ and his apostles, a baptism, is consistent only with its being immersion. The common and necessary use of a word meaning to immerse, and the marked distinction of this from sprinkling or pouring, would necessarily prevent its change from one to the others, or to meaning the use of a liquid, as some have maintained, "in any way."

If inspired writers had used the Greek word in another sense, surely the practice among Christians of immediately subsequent times would have corroborated this. But neither the Greeks, who are supposed best to understand their own language, nor the Latins, nor any barbarians, afford the slightest support to a supposed alteration by divine or any other warrant of the import of *baptize* and the words derived from it. Nor does Jewish proselyte baptism, whether it originated before, or, as many eminent Paedobaptists believe, after apostolic times, give the least countenance to anything short of immersion as baptism. The first recorded departure from immersion for baptism is an acknowledged deviation-an acknowledged imperfection-which, it was believed, required God's mercy and special necessity for its adoption. This took place at about the middle of the third century. Baptism was then believed requisite in order to have the certainty of salvation. A dying man might be incapable of being baptized. A substitute for baptism in such circumstances was admitted, with allowed disadvantages if life should be spared. This at length has been palmed off as baptism, as the very thing that God requires, or all that from any he demands! And while there is such a cross in being once immersed for Christ's sake, especially in these cold and northern regions, the convenience and decency of sprinkling are lauded to the skies. And by some who speak of immersion as if it could not be performed without a breach of delicacy, it is maintained that immersion is *one* of the actions embraced in the word divinely chosen when "baptizing" is enjoined.

The idea of necessary indecency in the "one immersion," or of danger unless in affliction, or special circumstances, the practice of our own land and other countries is continually and loudly condemning. Where danger or incapacity really prohibit, we believe God does not demand; but he authorizes no substitute in these circumstances. Nor is a more paltry subterfuge conceivable than that the sprinkling or pouring of a little water on the face is *substantially* baptizing a person. However great or little the importance we attach to baptism, we are bound, in observing it, to practise what God enjoins. For the servant of an earthly master to perform his own likings, instead of his master's biddings, it would be an insult which none would brook. The pretext for sprinkling and pouring that they are not forbidden, is a scandalizing of what God had enjoined, by choosing a human invention to the rejection of a divine appointment. If God is infinite in wisdom and love, a stern adherence to his precepts is our wisdom and profit. "This is the love of God, that we keep his commandments; and his commandments are not grievous."

On the *subjects* of baptism greater length, and some reference to our worthy author's erring assertions, are requisite. The divinely approved subjects of Christian baptism can be ascertained only from the New Testament. Christ's commission, confirmed as to its import by previous and especially by subsequent practice, and by every reference to this ordinance in the oracles of God, is "the law," and "the testimony." An attempt to prove the rightful subjects of Christian baptism from God's word and Jewish proselyte baptism, is to imitate the Popish appeal to Scripture and tradition. Besides, no man upon earth *knows* that proselyte baptism had an existence in apostolic times, whilst every one may know that its origin is "of men," not "from heaven;" and that the Bible alone is man's rule of faith and practice. Every legitimate inference from every part of Holy Writ we admit.

We maintain that the only proper subjects of Christian baptism are believers in Christ, those proselyted to Christ, disciples of Christ; or, since we have not, and are not required to have access to the heart, those who make a credible profession of faith in Christ. This we believe to be taught in the divine precept, "Go ye therefore, and teach [*make disciples of*] all nations, baptizing them in [*into*] the name of the Father, and of the Son, and of the Holy Ghost: teaching them to observe all things whatsoever I have commanded you;" and to be confirmed by the record, "Go ye into all the world, and preach the gospel to every creature, He that believeth and is baptized shall be saved; but he that believeth not shall be damned." We maintain the sufficiency of the first Scripture, independently of the latter, on which we lay not stress in this controversy, knowing that in some manuscripts it is wanting, yet believing with almost all our opponents, that it belongs to the word "by inspiration given." The first quoted passage, the commission of Christ for the guidance of his disciples, "unto the end of the world," does not say, first disciple, and then baptize, and then teach to observe all things, etc.; but that this is its import we maintain, from the construction of the entire precept, from what the apostles had before witnessed and practised, from their subsequent practice, and from every reference to baptism in their writings.

In understanding this passage, if we follow order, where, above all places, the most precise order might be expected, we must understand Christ's will to be, that we first make disciples, then baptize, etc. That order is not here to be regarded it devolves on the opponents of order to prove. In making disciples, the communication and the acceptance of truth, the teaching and the receiving of the good news, are requisite. After this and baptism, teaching is not to cease, "teaching them to observe all things whatsoever I have commanded you." Nor is there anything in the passage demanding another interpretation. It has indeed been said, that "them" after "baptizing" has "all nations" for its antecedent, that the discipling and baptizing are of equal extent, embracing the same persons, even every individual in all the nations; but that the discipling of all nations means the discipling of infants is no more apparent that infants are included where we are taught that all nations shall call our Redeemer blessed, or when he predicted, "Ye shall be hated of all nations." Nor is the antecedent, as maintained, although grammatically admissible, a grammatical requirement. Also, "that the inspired writers, any more than other men do not use the pronouns with such scrupulous exactness, is manifest" from an examination of the New Testament. It is however maintained, and by some who denounce immersion as inconvenient and dangerous, that the commission teaches that we are to make disciples by baptizing and teaching, these present participles, following the command to disciple, certainly including the *accomplishment* of the discipling, and necessarily involving a *contemporaneous* act. The word "by" is, however, no more in Christ's words than are firstly and secondly. The word "by," though frequently admissible in such sentences, without obscuring or altering the sense, is also frequently inadmissible, as involving the most obvious perversion of a writer's meaning. No one will doubt, on reading, "He spake, saying," etc., or, "They cried, saying," etc., that the speaking or crying is accomplished by *saying*; but when we read, "The men marvelled, saying" (Matt. 8:27), does any one doubt that the marvelling proceeded and caused the saying, and that the marvelling was not accomplished *by* the saying? When our Saviour said, "Lend, hoping for nothing again" (Luke 6:35), did he mean that the lending would be accomplished *by* hoping for nothing again? When we read, "Then came to him a man, kneeling down to him" (Matt. 17:14), do we understand that the coming to Christ was accomplished *by* kneeling, or that the kneeling was contemporaneous with the coming? No rule demands this absurdity. A thousand instances of such a construction in our own and the Greek language could be adduced as disproving the necessity of so understanding Christ's words. Moreover, were "by" admissible before the participles "baptizing" and "teaching," infants would be excluded as incapable of being taught; or if admitted because in them it is the first part of discipling, it must be continued, if baptizing and teaching are contemporaneous with discipling and the fulfilling of it, until the baptizing and teaching have unitedly accomplished the discipling. If the baptizing commenced as soon as convenient after birth, its continuance would be, as we maintain, until Christ should be in them "the hope of glory," until they became believers in Christ, or made a credible profession of this faith. Any rule that would unite the participle "baptizing" to the verb disciple, and make it the accomplishment of discipling and a contemporaneous act, would also unite the participle "teaching." Nor is there a noted Paedobaptist commentator, or controversialist, whom we remember, who does not interpret baptism *into the name of* Father, Son, and Spirit, baptism *into Christ,* or *into Moses,* as involving a profession and consecration; which interpretation necessarily excludes infants. Dr. Martensen says that "baptism, as a human ceremony, is an act of confession, by which a person is admitted into Christ's church;" that "the sacraments, as acts of the church, are chiefly to be viewed as acts of profession (*notos professionis*), visible, sensible acts, by participating in which, each person indeed confesses his Lord and the church." Mr. Watson says: "That Christ is formed in us (Gal. 4:19); that our nature is changed; that we are made holy and heavenly; this is to be baptized into Jesus. Rom. 6:3." He further speaks of an "oath of allegiance" which we make to God in baptism. Yet it is also said by him on Christ's commission, "The Greek is, 'Make disciples of all nations.' If it be asked, how should we make them *disciples*? It follows, 'Baptizing them and teaching them.' In a heathen nation, first teach, and then baptize them; but in a Christian church, first baptize, and then teach them" (p. 380). Not only has Christ given no intimation of two ways of discipling, not only do the inspired writings contain no record of apostolic discipling in two ways, but the very records of discipling and baptizing the heathen, as at Philippi and Corinth, are the records from which our opponents advocate their first baptizing, and then teaching.

We admit that in accordance with human phraseology, the word "disciples" is used in Scripture in application not only to those who were really, but also to those who were professedly disciples. Yet assuredly the Saviour did not wish his apostles, nor does he wish us, to make hypocrites; although, not having access to the heart, we may sometimes baptize the unworthy, as Philip baptized Simon. This inevitable fallibility we deem no more condemnable in ourselves than in the evangelist. From this necessary weakness of humanity, we may not only sometimes receive the unworthy to baptism and the Lord's Supper, but may also induct such into the highest office in the church of Christ. We are not justified for this reason in altering the import of a disciple of Christ, solemnly and explicitly given by the Saviour himself. The tendency of paedobaptism, as we could clearly show, is to pervert the import of a disciple of Christ, by teaching that an unconscious babe, that a child who can answer certain questions, yea, that a man or woman known to be ungodly, may, by baptism, become a disciple of Christ! Thus while certain conformists, maintaining justification by faith, are inconsistently teaching that baptism regenerates and converts into a child of God, certain nonconformists, maintaining the divine truth of salvation by grace through faith, teach that baptism disciples to Christ! A correct interpretation of *discipling* excludes infants from the commission.

According to this natural import of Christ's words; namely, that we are to disciple to him; to baptize into the name of Father, Son, and

Holy Spirit, and to teach obedience in all things to Christ's commands, we further conceive the apostles must have understood Christ, *on account of the baptism they had already witnessed and practised.* They knew not, so far as we are aware, any other baptism than John's, and that of Jesus through themselves. Were we to bind with the Bible all the Rabbinical lumber and all the condemned (or approved) Jewish traditions that the world contains, we should, while dishonou   g the sufficiency of inspired writ, be in the same destitution of evidence that the apostles knew of any other baptisms than those recorded in the oracles of God. John "baptized with the baptism *of repentance,* saying unto the people, that they should *believe on him who should come after him,* that is, on Christ Jesus (Acts 19:4). They "were baptized of him in Jordan, *confessing their sins*" (Mark 1:5). It was a baptism "into repentance," as this was the state professed by them while confessing their sins and being baptized. Until our Lord's commission, the Scriptures speak of no baptism from heaven in addition to John's, except that of Christ by means of his disciples. Concerning this the inspired record is, first, that "He baptized" (John 3:22), and secondly, that "He made and baptized more disciples than John, though Jesus himself baptized not, but his disciples" (John 4:1-2). He baptized *disciples.* He *made* AND baptized them. The instruction from this baptism can only be in favour of first making disciples, and then baptizing them. The whole of divine revelation respecting every baptism from heaven which the apostles had previously witnessed or practised, confirms our belief that they would certainly understand Christ's words according to their natural import already indicated.

We finally maintain that our view of the commission is correct, because the apostles so understood it, as their subsequent conduct and writings abundantly evidence. Peter, on the day of Pentecost, first preached the gospel of Christ, and then taught the anxiously enquiring to repent and be baptized in the name of Jesus Christ. They must change their minds, having been unbelieving in regard to Jesus as the Messiah and Saviour, and on this faith in Christ, to which God's Spirit was drawing and helping them, be baptized, thus in obedience to Christ, avowing their belief in him as the Messiah and their Saviour. And after further exhortation and instruction from Peter, "Then they that gladly received his word were baptized: and the same day there were added unto them about three thousand souls. And they continued steadfastly in the apostle's doctrine and fellowship, and in breaking of bread, and in prayers." The next record of baptism thus reads: "But when they believed Philip preaching the things concerning the kingdom of God and the name of Jesus Christ, they were baptized, both men and women. Then Simon himself believed also: and when he was baptized, he continued with Philip, and wondered, beholding the miracles and signs which were done." The next recorded baptism is that of the praying "brother Saul," whom the Lord had met on his way to Damascus. The next recorded baptism is that of Cornelius and "his kinsmen and near friends," of whose baptism Peter judged all would approve, since, while hearing Peter's words of divine instruction, the Lord had baptized them with the Holy Ghost, and they were heard to "speak with tongues, and magnify God." The next baptisms on record are those at Philippi and Corinth, adduced by Mr. Watson as proving that the apostles, in baptizing "whole families," baptized "little children" and "servants" (p. 381). We admit that, in Lydia's case, we have the record that "she was baptized, and her household," and the previous record respecting her, "whose heart the Lord opened, that she attended unto the things which were spoken of Paul" while nothing is said respecting the character of "her household." This proves not that Lydia had either husband or child. The household of this "seller of purple, of the city of Thyatire," might consist wholly of servants. Silence here neither proves nor confirms anything in favour of paedobaptism. Having no record respecting the character of this household, we are bound to believe that apostolic practice here accorded with previous and subsequent apostolic practice. The next baptism, that of the jailor "and all his," is one from which infants are clearly excluded. Paul and Silas "spake unto him the word of the Lord, and to all that were in his house;" and after baptism, "he set meat before them and rejoiced, believing (having believed) in God with all his house." The next record is equally explicit, and opposed to the baptism of infants or unbelievers. "And Crispus, the chief ruler of the synagogue, believed on the Lord, with all his house; and many of the Corinthians hearing, believed, and were bapitzed." The baptism of "certain disciples" at Ephesus, of whom we read, "And all the men were about twelve," equally refuses its aid to the baptism of infants; while "the household of Stephanas," of whom Paul says, "They have addicted themselves to the ministry of the saints," cannot be brought to the rescue of our opponents.

Arguments from references to baptism in God's word are as futile as those from precepts and examples in favour of baptizing infants. The apostle of the Gentiles appeals to all the "saints" in "Rome," that as "dead to sin," they had been "baptized into Jesus Christ," "baptized into his death," and "buried with him by baptism into death." Their having been baptized, demanded that they "should walk in newness of life." Is this applicable to infants? To the churches of Galatia he wrote, "For as many of you as have been baptized into Christ, have put on Christ." Of the Colossians he writes, "Buried with him in baptism, wherein also ye are risen with him through the faith of the operation of God, who hath raised him from the dead." The last mention of baptism is by Peter, who speaks of baptism as "the answer of a good conscience toward God." Thus condemnatory of paedobaptism is the entire New Testament.

But to another refuge the advocates of paedobaptism usually resort. Hence, in answer to the question, "How does it appear that children have a right to baptism?" we read, "Children are parties to the covenant of grace. The covenant was made with them. 'I will establish my covenant between me and thee, and thy seed after thee, for an everlasting covenant, to be a God unto thee, and to thy seed after thee,' Gen. 17:7. 'The promise is to you and to your children.' The covenant of grace may be considered either. 1. More strictly, as an absolute promise to give saving grace; and so none but the elect are in covenant with God. Or (2.) More largely, as a covenant containing in it many outward glorious privileges, in which respects the children of believers do belong to the covenant of grace," and "cannot justly be denied baptism, which is its seal. It is certain the children of believers were once visibly in covenant with God, and received the seal of their admission into the church. Where now do we find this covenant interest, or church membership of infants, repealed or made void? Certainly Jesus Christ did not come to put believers in a worse condition than they were in before. If the children of believers should not be baptized, they are in worse condition now than they were in before Christ's coming" (p. 380).

In this extract from Watson, God's gracious covenant with Abraham, or one of God's covenants with him, is styled "the covenant of grace." But the covenant of grace commenced with Adam, whether we restrict it to "the elect," those chosen to salvation, or regard it, "more largely," as referring to "outward glorious privileges." Again, God's covenant with Abraham was not a covenant with the elect of mankind, nor with the whole race, nor with Abraham and the elect descending from him, nor with Abraham and exclusively the children of believers, nor with any children for the sake of their parents, excepting Abraham's own children. Nor can the Pentecostal promise of Peter be proved to have any connection with, or reference to, the Abrahamic covenant, admitting that, as some promises resemble others, this and the immediately following may remind us of the predictions that in Abraham and his seed all the nations, all the families, of the earth shall be blessed. That all Abraham's descendants were elected to salvation, no one believes; nor is it less apparent that the children of wicked parents received the token of the covenant, as well as the children of believing parents; and in every instance beyond that of Abraham's children, not from filial relationship, but from relationship to Abraham. "The sons of David," as says Dr. Halley, "were circumcised according to the same law, and therefore, for the same reason as the sons of that worshipper of Baal, Ahab, and of that wicked woman, Jezebel." Nor was the covenant of God with Abraham and his seed a covenant with his seed as *infants*, but with his descendants. If the token of the covenant had been disobediently neglected, it might at any age, and irrespective of character in its recipient or the parent, be performed from relationship to Abraham. Not one of Abraham's natural seed is another Abraham, nor is one believer. But all believers may be spoken of as the (believing) children of faithful Abraham. That God graciously entered into covenant with all Abraham's descendants for his sake, and instituted a sign to be fixed on every male, is no evidence that God has entered into covenant with the natural children of every believer, and with each child, for the parent's sake, and that the baptism of male and female *infants* of believers is the appointed sign of this covenant. Where is such a law but in the writings of Paedobaptists?

The "covenant interest" of "the children of believers" as such, or of "infants" of believers, or the "church membership of infants," and "the seal of their admission into the church," giving to the word "church" any idea resembling its New Testament use in application to the church, or a church of Christ, needed not to be "repealed or made void," because they had never existed. If God's covenanting with Abraham and his seed, and instituting the sign of circumcision in males, proves the church membership of the seed of Abraham, it proves an Ishmaelitish as well as an Israelitish church of God, and a church to which ungodly adults, equally with the infants of believers, belonged. If circumcision is the *seal of admission into the church*, there has been not only a Jewish church, but an Edomite, a Moabite, and Ammonite church. Did Episcopalians and all others who believe a church of Christ to be "a *congregation* of *faithful* men," always speak consistently with this, we should hear less of any *nation* at any period, or of any *building* in any place, as a church. Why should we not, except where the idea of assembly exists, after the manner of inspired writers, speak of those who anciently enjoyed the divine favour, as saints, as the people of God, as those that feared the Lord, as the righteous, etc., instead of confoundingly speaking of the church before the flood, the patriarchal, the Abrahamic, the Mosaic, the Jewish (etc.) church?

The children of believers, if not baptized, are not in "a worse condition" than were the circumcised children of believers before the Christian dispensation. Grace is not, and never was, hereditary. The "sons of God" have ever been those "born, not of blood, nor of the will of the flesh, nor of the will of man, but of God." In every age have men become "the children of God by faith." This faith has been stronger, and has shone more conspicuously and gloriously, in some than in others; but "without faith it is impossible to please" God, and it ever has been (Heb. 11:6, etc.). The application of this to those only who are capable of believing, none can doubt. It is equally clear that the faith of some must have had reference to a Messiah to come, and of others to a Messiah who had appeared. We doubt not that the children of believers, they and their parents being spared, have had, and to the end of prevailing and parental ungodliness will have, advantages not possessed by the children of unbelievers. Parental piety superadded to parental affection necessitates this. Nor can there be hindrance-we shall not now speak of the encouragement and help-from him who has left it on record, "Train up a child in the way he should go: and when he is old, he will not depart from it." There is not however the slightest intimation in God's word that "the children of believers," or "the infant seed of believers," in distinction from the children or infant seed of unbelievers, constitute or belong to "the election of grace." The attempt to found such an hypothesis on the covenant with Abraham and his seed, requires the belief that grace is hereditary; that all Abraham's posterity were in infancy the children of God and heirs of heaven *through their relationship to Abraham,* whatever their subsequent piety or ungodliness, salvation or damnation; that divine grace through Abraham naturally and efficaciously descended through all his seed, or, if it is preferred, through all his seed in the line of Isaac and Jacob, until the coming of Christ, when the infant seed of believers have the same "claim to the covenant of grace as their parents; and having a right to the covenant, they cannot justly be denied baptism." What inference is possible from this reasoning, but that the infant seed of all from Abraham to Christ, who descended not from Abraham, were heirs of hell? And that it is now, and from the time of Christ has been, the condition of all infants having unbelieving parents? Besides, unless circumcision introduced into the covenant of grace, or confirmed spiritual blessings, or promoted spiritual along with its temporal good, and unless the baptism of infants secures temporal or spiritual good to the same extent, which also the lack of baptism by infants prevents, the implied retaining of the same blessings since by baptism, and the inferred diminution of blessings by the omitted infant baptism, fall to the ground. We might also inquire of some, Can the blessings of the covenant, to those born in the covenant, and who have its blessings signed and sealed to them, slip out of their hands?

It has probably been reserved to Dr. Bushnell, while saying many good things on parental influence and obligations, in advocating the baptism of infants, to carry filial relationship and its effects to their most absurd and monstrous extent. He teaches, in his *Christian Nurture,* that "until the child comes to his will, we must regard him still as held within the matrix of the parental life" (p. 97); that the covenant with Abraham "was a family covenant, in which God engaged to be the God of the seed as of the father. And the seal of the covenant was a seal of *faith*, applied to the whole house, as if the continuity of faith were somehow to be, or somehow might be, maintained in a line that is parallel with the continuity of sin in the family" (p. 106); that "the old rite of proselyte baptism, which made the families receiving it Jewish citizens and children of Abraham, was applied over directly to the Christian uses, and the rite went by households " (p. 107); that by "organic unity in families," we have "the only true solution of the Christian church and of baptism as related to membership" (p. 108); that "baptism is applied to the child on the ground of its organic unity with the parent, imparting and pledging a grace to sanctify that unity, and make it good in the field of religion: (p. 110); and that the child is *potentially* regenerate, being regarded as existing in connection with powers and causes that *contain* the fact before time, and separate from time" (p. 110). Thus the "seal of *faith*" has belonged to infants and unbelievers, and now belongs, and is restricted to, believers and their children! If Jewish "proselyte baptism" is made "over directly to the Christian uses," this is, of course, taught in God's word, or we are expressly or by implication taught, that the Jewish Talmud, a Rabbinical composition of the third century of the Christian era, belongs wholly, or in some specified part, to the oracles of God! We deny not "an organic unity" in any man, or any animal, having head, heart, lungs, liver, etc.; nor do we deny a union between Christ and his people, so that he lives in them; but we deny a union between children and parents, so that when father or mother is converted, the child becomes "a new creature," or becomes then, and not before, "potentially regenerate." We maintain that man becomes potentially regenerate, not through organic unity with any believing man, but as belonging to those for whom God has instituted an economy of grace, no man becoming potentially regenerate but through the sacrifice of the Son of God, which atones for sin and secures the bestowment of the divine Spirit. Well may Dr. B. piteously exclaim on his "doctrine of organic unity," "as a ready solvent for the rather perplexing difficulties of this difficult subject," that "one difficulty remains, namely, that so few can believe it" (p. 111). There is as much evidence that a child is baptized in the baptism of the parent, as that it is regenerated in the regeneration of the parent; yea, that the whole life and character of the child, and its eternal salvation or damnation, are that of the parent.

We believe that the circumcision, not only of male adults, but of male *infants*, was divinely enjoined, and that the unconsciousness of the latter constituted no hindrance to an accomplishment of the design of this institution; and we doubt not God's right, if he had seen it good, to institute a rite under the Christian dispensation that should embrace the unconscious, both males and females; but we deny the shadow of evidence that he has so enacted. The existence of circumcision from Abraham proves it not. Nor are we taught that baptism is in the place of circumcision, although in some things there is a resemblance in one to the other. The antitype of circumcision, or spiritual, Christian circumcision, is the renewal of the heart. Rom. 2:28-29; I Cor. 7:19; Gal. 6:15; Phil. 3:3; Col. 2:11. The apostles and elders gathered together at Jerusalem to consider the necessity of circumcision, which some of the baptized Jewish believers maintained, drop not a single hint to the erring that baptism is in the place of circumcision. The apostle of the Gentiles, warning the Colossian believers, and rebuking those in the churches of Galatia who held the destructive error, instead of teaching that baptism occupies the place of circumcision, teaches that Christian circumcision, the circumcision of Christ, is a circumcision "without hands, in putting off the body of the sins of the flesh." Nor is there in the fact that all children, or all the children of believers, are of "the kingdom of God," a particle of evidence that God has commanded their baptism. The Scriptures which speak of baptism, recording its appointment, its practice, its nature, design, or benefit, are those from which its divinely approved subjects can be learned. These speak of confession of sin, repentance, faith in Christ, discipleship, a good conscience, as characteristic of the baptized. Not a word is recorded respecting parents or others as proxies for "the child's personal engagement" (p. 381). Ourselves, our children, and all we possess, are God's property; and with all as "his servants," God has a sovereign right to deal. The duty of baptism is not learnt from this fact, but from the revelation of God's will. The apostle Paul, speaking of the marriage bond, when one partner has become a Christian, and the other remains an unbeliever, teaches a sacredness in the children and the unbelieving partner that forbids a dissolution of the connection; but, while attributing the same holiness to the children and the unbelieving partner, he says not a syllable implying a "right and title to baptism" (p. 382). Everything really included in parental dedication is as much the privilege of the Baptist as Paedobaptist. It is a benefit to the child when no deceptive substitute has been performed on him, preventing, or helping to prevent, his personal, conscious, voluntary, and acceptable obedience to God's command. The obtaining by infants, through baptism, of entrance into the church, of "a right sealed to the ordinances," that is, to the Lord's Supper, etc., and of "the tutelage of angels to be the infant's lifeguard," may be in the imagination of Paedobaptists; but these are not in the word of God, any more than that baptism is to elected infants "a 'seal of the righteousness of faith,' a laver of regeneration, and a badge of adoption" (p. 380). Not only are the Scriptures silent respecting infant baptism, but every record relating to baptism forbids its existence in apostolic times, and its right to a subsequent existence. Nor does Irenaeus, or any of the earliest fathers, say one word favouring the supposition of its existence, notwithstanding the inference that is drawn by some of the Paedobaptists from one passage in Irenaeus. What authority has a practice that can but be proved as possibly beginning to exist at the close of the second, or in the early part of the third century? For Tertullian, dissuading from the baptism of children, may not refer to infants. The existence of infant baptism in the third century is certain. The existence in the third, and in the preceding century, of sentiments on the efficacy of baptism, and of various practices which have no foundation in Holy Writ, is easily and abundantly proved. But neither infant baptism nor any other practice could be sanctioned by evidence of existence in the age immediately succeeding the apostolic period, or existence in apostolic times, if destitute of apostolic sanction; and especially if opposed to, and destructive of, what is divinely enjoined. The fact that inspired writers, in recording baptisms, except where the baptism of parents and other members of the family take place at the same time, say nothing as to parental piety, accords with and corroborates our view of baptism as a personal and voluntary profession and engagement. Every record of baptisms in Holy Writ, and every reference to baptism, is a confirmation of believers' baptism as the "one baptism" for parents and children, for every generation, and for all alike, to the end of time.

Nor are we ashamed of the Baptist, as compared with the Paedobaptist history, tracing it through every age, and in every country, from apostolic to the present times, although we are not disposed to boast of our own righteousness. We justify not "the doings of the Anabaptists in Germany," though Paedobaptists were united with them, and all were then but emerging from the darkness and errors of Popery. We believe in what has just fallen from the lips of the Rev. W. Walters respecting the Baptists of this country. " 'From the beginning,' says Locke, 'they were the friends and advocates of absolute liberty-just and true liberty, equal and impartial liberty.' The claim which we make to have

been the first expositors and advocates in modern times of religiou
liberty, is based on the surest foundation, and is capable of the mos
satisfactory proof." Instead of exalting believers' baptism above measure
we say in the words of our honourable and Rev. brother Noel, "It is no
separation from the church of Rome, or from the church of England, no
a scriptural organisation, or evangelical doctrine, which can alone secur
our Saviour's approbation." They who speak of infant baptism as
putting of the child's name in a will by the parent, need to be reminde
of God's prerogative, and of the character of his government as reveale
in the words: "All souls are mine; as the soul of the father, so also th
soul of the son is mine: the soul that sinneth, it shall die." Who, believin
this testimony, can also believe that unbaptized infants are "suckin
pagans," while those kindly bapitzed through parental influence ar
sucking Christians? The baptism of believers, we believe to be
reasonable, scriptural, and profitable service, calculated to strengthen an
perpetuate every right feeling and conduct. But in whatever esteem w
hold the erring Paedobaptist, and however cordially we say, and hope eve
to say, "Grace be with all them that love our Lord Jesus Christ i
sincerity," we are obliged to think and speak of infant baptism accordin
to a writer before quoted. "In it there is no conscience, no will, n
reasonable service. It allies persons without their consent, or even thei
intelligence, to a religious creed; it forces upon them an unreasoning an
unwilling service; it imposes upon them an unconscious profession; i
anticipated the conduct of riper years to a degree which both nature an
Scripture condemn; and is therefore a violation of their just rights."

❑ *The Children of Church Members* by Richard Furman
This reprint discusses both the relationship of the children of church members and raising such children in the discipline and admonition of the Lord. Dr. Timothy George, Dean of Beeson Divinity School says, "I am delighted to recommend this timely republication of Richard Furman's classic statement on Christian Nurture...This classic resource from the historic Reformed Baptist tradition will be an asset to godly parents everywhere." (20 pp.)

❑ *Baptism and Church Communion* by John Bunyan
John Bunyan, the seventeenth century author of *Pilgrim's Progress*, known as a "Baptist," wrote several small treatises on baptism arguing for accepting those into church communion who have a conscientious difference on the matter, namely the Reformed paedobaptists (infant baptists). As Bunyan says, "I own water baptism to be God's ordinance, but I make no idol of it." (20 pp.)

❑ *Does Baptism Means Immersion?* by Tom Wells
In this succinct treatise the author addresses the single issue of the mode of baptism. He does so by answering various objections that have historically been raised against immersion. (29 pp.)